NI Key Stage 3

English Year **8**

NI Key Stage 3
English Year **8**

Series Editor: **Kate O'Hanlon**

Authors: **Noreen Doran**, **Vanessa Goucher**, **Maura Johnston** and **Jennifer Magowan**

Hodder Murray
A MEMBER OF THE HODDER HEADLINE GROUP

The Publishers would like to thank the following for permission to reproduce copyright material:

Photo credits Author's own, p.6; Banana Stock/Photolibrary.com, p. 43; Kindra Clineff/Photolibrary.com, p. 47; Cover illustration © 2005 Walker Books Ltd. From *Skeleton Key* by Anthony Horowitz. Boy with torch logo™ & © 2006 Stormbreaker Productions Ltd. Reproduced by permission of Walker Books Ltd, London SE11 5HJ, p. 80; Theo Kingma/Rex Features, p. 88

Acknowledgements p.8 *First Day at School* © Roger McGough 1976 reproduced by permission of PFD (www.pfd.co.uk) on behalf of Roger McGough; pp.10–11 *A Rhinoceros, Some Ladies and a Horse* by James Stephens in Modern Irish Short Stories by Frank O'Connor (Oxford University Press, 1957); p.15 from *Portrait of the Artist as a Young Girl* edited by John Quinn © RTE 1985, reprinted by permission of the Random House Group Ltd; p.18 from *The Day I Fell Down the Toilet and Other Poems* by Steve Turner (© Lion Publishing, 1997); p.23 from *Jenny Bristow's Country Cooking 2*, © Appletree Press; p.24 from *Electric Light* by Seamus Heaney (© Faber and Faber, 2001); p.28 from *All of Us There* by Polly Devlin (© Virago Press, 2003); p.35 extract 1: from *The Stolen Child* by WB Yeats, printed by permission of AP Watt Ltd on behalf of Gráinne Yeats, Executrix of the Estate of Michael Butler Yeats; p.35 extract 3: *This is Just to Say* by William Carlos Williams, from COLLECTED POEMS: 1909–1939, VOLUME I, edited by Christopher MacGowan, copyright © 1938 by New Directions Publishing Corp. Reprinted by permission of New Directions Publishing Corp & Carcanet Press Limited; p.36 from *Limericks* by Michael Palin, published by Red Fox, reprinted by permission of The Random House Group Ltd; p.39 by Pie Corbett, from *Rice, Pie and Moses* by John Rice, Pie Corbett and Brian Moses (Macmillan Children's Books, 1995); p.39 © Donna Brock; p.39 © Philip Adams; p.41 © Jill Campbell; p.46 by John Rice, from *Rice, Pie and Moses* by John Rice, Pie Corbett and Brian Moses (© Macmillan Children's Books, 1995); pp.54–56 extract from *Sisters...No Way!* by Siobhán Parkinson published by the O'Brien Press Ltd, Dublin, © Siobhán Parkinson; p.57 & p.58 from *Shadow of the Beast* by Maggie Pearson (Hodder Children's Books, 2002), reprinted by permission of Hodder and Stoughton Limited © Hodder and Stoughton Limited; p.72–73 *Ladies First* from *Free To Be ... You And Me* by Shel Silverstein Copyright © 1981, Evil Eye, Music. By permission of Edite Kroll Literary Agency Inc; p.80 cover illustration © 2005 Walker Books Ltd, boy with torch logo™ & © Stormbreaker Productions Ltd, reproduced by permission of Walker Books Ltd, London SE11 5HJ); p.82 & p.84 from *Skeleton Key* by Anthony Horowitz © 2002 Anthony Horowitz, reproduce by permission of Walker Books Ltd, London SE11 5HJ; p.86 from *Two Points to Murder* by Carolyn Keene (© Simon & Schuster, 1987).

Every effort has been made to trace all copyright holders, but if any have been inadvertently overlooked the Publishers will be pleased to make the necessary arrangements at the first opportunity.

Although every effort has been made to ensure that website addresses are correct at time of going to press, Hodder Murray cannot be held responsible for the content of any website mentioned in this book. It is sometimes possible to find a relocated web page by typing in the address of the home page for a website in the URL window of your browser.

Hodder Headline's policy is to use papers that are natural, renewable and recyclable products and made from wood grown in sustainable forests. The logging and manufacturing processes are expected to conform to the environmental regulations of the country of origin.

Orders: please contact Bookpoint Ltd, 130 Milton Park, Abingdon, Oxon OX14 4SB. Telephone: (44) 01235 827720. Fax: (44) 01235 400454. Lines are open 9.00–5.00, Monday to Saturday, with a 24-hour message answering service. Visit our website at www.hoddereducation.co.uk

First published in 2007 by
Hodder Murray, an imprint of Hodder Education,
a member of the Hodder Headline Group,
an Hachette Livre UK Company,
338 Euston Road
London NW1 3BH

Impression number	5	4	3	2
Year	2010	2009	2008	2007

Cover photo © Michael St Maur Sheil/Corbis
Illustrations by Barking Dog Art
Typeset in 11 on 14 pt Helvetica Light by Phoenix Photosetting, Chatham, Kent
Printed in Italy

A catalogue record for this title is available from the British Library

ISBN: 978 0340 87684 8

Contents

Unit 1: You and your language

Unit 2: Our environment

Unit 3: Rhyme and reason

Unit 4: The reader's point of view

Contents

Introduction

Welcome to your English textbook for Year 8, specially written for young people in Northern Ireland. We hope you will enjoy building on your language skills and knowledge by engaging with the exciting texts and activities provided in this book.

This textbook will support your English programme as part of the Revised Northern Ireland Curriculum for Key Stage 3, but we anticipate that it will also develop language skills that will be useful across the curriculum. Remember to make use of your language skills and knowledge when working in other subjects.

The textbook has eight units that are arranged so that language experiences and skills may be established and consolidated. However, we hope that you will explore the variety of English beyond these materials in your talking and listening, wide reading, and writing for different purposes and audiences.

Kate O'Hanlon, Noreen Doran, Vanessa Goucher, Maura Johnston, and Jennifer Magowan

Learning Intentions for English

Learning Outcomes	Words used to describe learning outcomes in English
Managing information	Research and manage information effectively, using Mathematics and ICT where appropriate
Thinking, problem solving, decision making	Show deeper understanding by thinking critically and flexibly, solving problems and making informed decisions, using Mathematics and ICT where appropriate
Being creative	Demonstrate creativity and initiative when developing ideas and following them through
Working with others	Work effectively with others
Self-management	Demonstrate self-management by working systematically, persisting with tasks, evaluating and improving own performance

Features of the book

Beginning work

Each unit will show two boxes at the top of the page:
- What we will be doing
- What we will be learning.
These will make clear the purposes of each unit.

Writing

It will help if you are clear about the following:
Purpose: Why am I writing? What **genre** of writing will be suitable for my purpose – recount, instruction, explanation, narrative?

Audience: to whom or for whom am I writing? What form of writing will be most suitable – letter, diary, story, email, video, news article, magazine?

Word definitions

In many places you will find dictionary definitions of the words used in that part of the book. This will help you get on quickly and successfully with the work you are doing.

Talking and listening

Many activities will ask you to work in pairs or small groups. This will help you to learn and think more successfully.

ICT

We hope you will pick up and develop suggestions made about the use of:
- computers
- software
- the internet
- film
- video/DVD
- audio texts
- radio.

Reading

Texts in a wide range of genres and forms will be provided. Let them motivate you to read more. You may be guided by suggestions made for extended reading.

Self-assessment

At the end of each unit you will be asked:
- What have you learned?
- What are your next goals for improvement?
This will help develop your skills.

Developing your thinking

You will be given many opportunities to think about your own thinking processes and skills. The work will ask you to be a creative and critical thinker. Problem solving will be an element of each unit of work.

Unit 1: You and your language

What we will be doing

In this unit we will:

- talk about the origins of your speech, reading and writing
- read about others' first language experiences
- think about the ways writers present early language and experiences, and compare texts
- build up a portfolio of written work including early memories and short autobiographical and biographical pieces.

What we will be learning

In this unit we will learn:

- how our language develops from early baby language, with help from our early reading
- how to use the skills of writing in the recount genre
- how to develop a number of ways to help yourself get better at spelling
- how to work with others to collaborate in a group.

Thinking skills and personal capabilities

In this unit we will:

- listen and respond to others in a group
- read and explore meaning in a group
- review your own and others' writing
- work to reach agreement in groups.

Introduction

Have you ever wondered about how and why you first communicated? In this unit you are going to think about how you first spoke and read, and compare this with others' experiences. It will be interesting to work out if this has an effect on how you communicate today.

Who are you?

Your name is important: it is often the first thing other people will know about you, or the first thing your parents say to you. It can reveal a lot about you and your background. Task 1 looks at where our names came from.

 ## Task 1

In this task you will:

* talk together in small groups.

Here are some questions to get you thinking and to help you find out everything you can about the meaning of the names of the people in your group:

1   Do you know who named you and why your names were chosen? (Think about your first name and any other names you might have, e.g. your Christening name, nicknames, etc.)

2   Do you know if your name has a meaning?

3   Is your name from another language?

4   Has there been a time when your name has been wrongly used?

5   Do different people have different names for you (e.g. grandparents, younger brother/sister)?

6   What do you prefer to be called and why?

Task 2

In this task you will:

- share ideas with a partner.

To help others to find out more about who you are, draw around your hand. Inside the outline include as much information about yourself as you can fit in, or that you want to tell someone else. You could share it with a partner or with your group. This is a very short autobiography, or a written description of yourself.

Early speech

Your early speech

Your speech can reveal a lot about you. Most parents will have stories about what it was like when you were a toddler and learning to speak. You are going to write a piece of personal writing called 'My early speech'. As preparation, here are some research questions. Ask someone at home, who has known you since you were a baby, to help you answer the questions.

1   When did you start saying words?
2   What was your first word?
3   Did anyone record your early speech on video or cassette? Bring it in to share.
4   Did you have a word that you always pronounced wrongly? Why do you think you did this?
5   Are there any other languages spoken in your house? Why is this?
6   Does your family have any accent or dialect phrases?

Task 3

In this task you will:

- reflect on your earliest memories.

Write the most interesting things you used to say when you were little in the first pages of your Writing Portfolio (see page 17) under the heading, 'My early speech'.

Roger McGough has written a poem in which he speaks in the voice of a student on their first day at school, a boy who can't even remember his own name. He has used some words that are examples of early speech. As you read it, think about whether he has captured the experience well.

First Day At School

A millionbillionwillion miles from home
Waiting for the bell to go. (To go where?)
Why are they all so big, other children,
So noisy? So much at home they
must have been born in uniform.
Lived all their lives in playgrounds.
Spent the years inventing games
that don't let me in. Games
that are rough, that swallow you up.

And the railings.
All around, the railings.
Are they to keep out wolves and monsters?
Things that carry off and eat children?
Things you don't take sweets from?
Perhaps they're to stop us getting out.
Running away from the lessins. Lessins.
What does a lessin look like?
Sounds small and slimy.
They keep them in glassrooms.
Whole rooms made out of glass. Imagine.

I wish I could remember my name.
Mummy said it would come in useful.
Like wellies. When there's puddles.
Yellowwellies. I wish she was here.
I think my name is sewn on somewhere.
Perhaps the teacher will read it for me.
Tea-cher. The one who makes the tea.

'First Day At School' by Roger McGough

 **Task 4**

In this task you will:

*   explore Roger McGough's poem.

1   The poet, Roger McGough, uses some words in the poem opposite that could be called 'baby language'. Underline these.

2   The child in the poem does not understand some adult words. The misunderstandings make the reader laugh. Underline these words in another colour. (You may find three.)

3   Do you remember your first day at primary school? Do you think that Roger McGough has written about it well?

4   Write down a memory you have from primary school when you felt that you were on your own. You can create something if you don't remember anything appropriate.

Spelling

In the poem, 'First Day At School', the poet deliberately spells some words wrongly, to show that the person in the poem is a young person. Do you spell words wrongly sometimes? What happens when you do? Here are some things that you can do to help:

> **Step 1** Make a list of the errors you have made in your workbooks in the past that have been pointed out by your teachers or by a writing partner.
>
> **Step 2** Go over this list and try to see if there are any patterns in the mistakes, for example, endings, plurals, tenses.
>
> **Step 3** Check with a dictionary for the correct spellings.
>
> **Step 4** Set a target for improving these words.
>
> **Step 5** Try different strategies for learning the correct spellings, for example, sounding out the syllables.

As you read the next extract, from 'A Rhinoceros, Some Ladies, and a Horse' by James Stephens, think about how this writer has captured the experience of being a child. The story is set in Victorian Ireland in the world of Charles Stewart Parnell, music-halls and horse-drawn carriages, and 11-year-old James is already at work.

A Rhinoceros, Some Ladies, and a Horse

One day, in my first job, a lady fell in love with me. It was quite unreasonable, of course, for I wasn't wonderful: I was small and thin, and I weighed much the same as a largish duck-egg. I didn't fall in love with her, or anything like that. I got under the table, and stayed there until she had to go wherever she had to go to.

[…]

The place I was working at was, amongst other things, a theatrical agency. I used to be sitting in a corner of the office floor, waiting to be told to run somewhere and back.

[…]

One day a great lady of the halls came in and was received on the knee. She was very great. Her name was Maudie Darling, or thereabouts. My bosses called her nothing but 'Darling', and she called them the same. When the time came for her to arrive the whole building got palpitations of the heart. After waiting a while my thin boss got angry, and said – 'Who does the woman think she is? If she isn't here in two twos I'll go down to the entry, and when she does come I'll boot her out.' The fat boss said – 'She's only two hours late, she'll be here before the week's out.'

Within a few minutes there came great clamours from the courtyard. Patriotic cheers, such as Parnell himself never got, were thundering. My bosses ran instantly to the inner office. Then the door opened, and the lady appeared.

She was very wide, and deep, and magnificent. She was dressed in camels and zebras and goats: she had two peacocks in her hat and a rabbit muff in her hand, and she strode among these with prancings. […]

And then … she saw me! […] She swept my two bosses right away from her, and she became a kind of queen, very glorious to behold: but sad, startled. She stretched a long, slow arm out and out and out and then she unfolded a long, slow finger, and pointed it at me – 'Who is THAT??' she whispered in a strange whisper that could be heard two miles off.

My fat boss was an awful liar – 'The cat brought that in,' said he.

But the thin boss rebuked him: 'No,' he said, 'it was not the cat. Let me introduce you; darling, this is James. James, this is the darling of the gods.'

'And of the pit,' said she, sternly.

She looked at me again. Then she sank to her knees and spread out both arms to me –

'Come to my Boozalum, angel,' said she in a tender kind of way.

I knew what she meant, and I knew that she didn't know how to pronounce that word. I took a rapid glance at the area indicated. The lady had a boozalum you could graze a cow on. I didn't wait one second, but slid, in one swift, silent slide, under the table. Then she came forward and said a whole lot of poems to me under the table, imploring me, among a lot of odd things, to 'come forth, and gild the morning with my eyes', but at last she was reduced to whistling at me with two fingers in her mouth, the way you whistle for a cab.

I learned after she had gone that most of the things she said to me were written by a poet fellow named Spokeshave. They were very complimentary, but I couldn't love a woman who mistook my old bosses for boys, and had a boozalum that it would take an Arab chieftain a week to trot across on a camel.

From 'A Rhinoceros, Some Ladies, and a Horse' by James Stephens

 Task 5

In this task you will:

- examine the language used by James Stephens in his short story.

1   What things does the boy remember vividly from his experience? Think about: people, names, sights, sounds and feelings.

2   James Stephens describes them from a young person's point of view. Underline the words which show that the narrator thought about things differently than the adults in the scene.

3   Pick out your favourite childish descriptions. Why did you choose these?

4   Can you remember any embarrassing incidents from your childhood?

Task 6: Two little boys – comparison of two texts

In this task you will:

- find similarities and differences.

1   Both the texts that you have read have been describing early experiences and memories of two young boys. Both writers have chosen to write using childish expressions. On a chart like the one below, record features of each of the texts. Some examples are shown to help you.

	The poem	The short story
The central character	*4-year-old boy*	
The setting		*A theatrical agency*
The language used		
Features that made it seem realistic	*Children's games* *Railings around the playground*	

2   Think about how the poem by Roger McGough and the extract from James Stephens' short story are similar and how they are different. Which of the two texts did you prefer and why?

Task 7

In this task you will:

- plan and write a recount.

You are going to write a piece of **recount** writing to tell the audience something about your experience as a new student.

Planning

1 Make a list of all the new things and experiences that a student has to cope with on either their first day at primary school or at secondary school. Select which of these you want to write about.

2 Organise the order of events, starting with the earliest event in the day.

3 Plan your paragraphs according to the sequence that works best.

Remember, features of recount writing include:

- use of emotive language to convey the event effectively
- use of precise details and vocabulary to record the event accurately
- use of first or third person depending on whether it is your story or another's
- use of simple past tense, i.e. 'The teacher smiled'
- use of words to link events, i.e. '*later* that morning…'

4 Now write your recount, 'My first day at school'.

Early reading

Having looked at your early speech in Task 3, let's turn to your early reading. Do you remember learning to read? Was it at home, before starting school, or was it in a primary school class? What were your first reading books like? Task 8 helps you to reflect on some of those books and to see whether you can find things that they have in common.

 **Task 8**

In this task you will:

- think about and discuss books you have enjoyed.

Here are some ideas to get you thinking about your early reading:

1   As a group of three or four, think about the books you first read and those you most enjoyed.

2   The best books that we have read are ....

3   A good children's book is ....

4   Talk about:

- **presentation:** they look like .... (colour, drawings, etc.)
- **types of story:** they are about .... (children, animals)
- **language used:** they are written .... they are funny because ...
- **font used:** they use capital letters, different sizes of print in the following way ....

5   Compare the books with **comics**. Which are better and why?

6   If you are allowed, bring your books into school to make a display.

Evaluation of working with others

How well did you work as a group to discuss this topic? Ask yourself some of these questions:

- Did you say what you wanted to say?
- Do you think the others understood what you said to them?
- How do you know they understood you?
- How did you feel towards other members of the group who held very different views from you?
- Are you pleased/very pleased/not pleased with the outcomes of your group work?

Next time you have the opportunity to work with others, think about how you could improve your contribution.

Readers around us

You have been discussing what the rest of your group thinks about reading, and at what age they first started to read. This next extract describes how Joan Lingard, a well-known Irish writer, began to read. Think about how her experience is similar or different from your own.

Portrait of the Artist as a Young Girl

I could never get enough to read and I'm sure that's why I ultimately became a writer. The local library was quite far away, so I couldn't go there on my own when I was young. It appeared to me then to be like an old shed; and in fact when I went back there again recently it still looked like that! The books then were very tattered and ancient. They had long since lost their dust jackets and their spines had a greasy feeling about them. The pages were filthy, spattered with egg and tomato ketchup. I hated the feel of those books so much that I used to turn the pages with a postcard and cover the spine with paper wrapper – but that did not thwart my love of the books themselves. I read absolutely everything I was allowed to read in the junior library – you weren't allowed into the senior section until you were fourteen. I read all the books that children have loved for years – the 'Chalet School' books, Enid Blyton, *Just William*, *Biggles* – and when my mother would ask me what I wanted for Christmas I always demanded a book. One Christmas I got eight books and I had read them all before I went to bed that night! My mother was beginning to despair of keeping me supplied with books and finally one day, when I was moaning, 'I've got nothing to read, I'm bored!', she turned to me and said, 'Why don't you go away and write your own book!' That was how I began as a writer, at the age of eleven.

From Portrait of the Artist as a Young Girl
edited by John Quinn

Task 9

In this task you will:

- share your reactions to Joan Lingard's story.

1   What evidence can you find in Joan Lingard's account to show that she was enthusiastic about reading?

2   Describe in your own words what the library books were like – appearance and texture.

3   Which were Joan Lingard's favourite children's books? Have you heard of any of them?

4   Why did Joan Lingard start to write books?

5   Is there anything similar about Joan Lingard's experience of books and yours?

Early writing

Reading can be an adventure, taking you into a world of other people, created by them. What about the worlds *you* can create? Let us turn our attention to writing. We write for all sorts of reasons, not just to tell stories, and for all kinds of audiences. When did you first learn to write? How did you learn your letters? Did you have any difficulty making your writing neat?

Autobiography

When we write about ourselves, it can be real and authentic. This is called our **autobiography**. When famous people want us to know what sort of life they have had, they sometimes write an autobiography. The extract in the previous section from *A Portrait of the Artist as a Young Girl* is autobiographical.

Biography

If someone writes a story about another person's life, that is a **biography**.

Task 10

In this task you will:

- create a biography.

1   Use a digital camera, if the school has one, or a disposable camera to take a photo of someone in your class.

2   While waiting for the photo to be developed or printed, interview the person for a short biography to be displayed beside the photo. You could use their 'hand autobiography' if they did one earlier in Task 2. Interesting things to ask your friend can include questions about their hobbies, pets, favourite team or band, where their name came from, their favourite book or film. Think of good questions to find out as much as you can. Write this up in a few points or a paragraph.

3   When your photo is developed, add the description to it and put together a display for the classroom, or your form room, if you have one.

 Task 11

In this task you will:

- review the work covered in Unit 1.

Writing Portfolio

Finally, put together a portfolio on 'My language autobiography' including what you learned about the origins of your name, your first words, your favourite books (if any!), your response to the poems and extracts in the unit, and an evaluation of what you have learned and the skills you have developed.

  Task 12: Words

In this task you will:

- prepare to perform a poem
- think about the power of words.

This task focuses on a poem that is a celebration of the words we use, whether in writing, reading or speaking. Read the poem. You will be asked to try to perform the poem in a group, so think about how you might do that.

I Like Words

I like words
Do you like words?
Words aren't hard to find:
Words on walls and words in books,
Words deep in your mind.

Words in jokes
That make you laugh
Words that seem to smell.
Words that end up inside out,
Words you cannot spell.

Words that fly
And words that crawl,
Words that screech and bump.
Words that glide and words that swing,
Words that bounce and jump.

Words that paint
And words that draw,
Words that make you grin.
Words that make you shake and sweat,
Words that touch your skin.

Words of love
That keep you warm,
Words that make you glad.
Words that hit you, words that hurt,
Words that make you sad.

Words in French
And words in slang,
Words like 'guy' and 'dude'
Words you make up, words you steal,
Words they say are rude.

I like words
Do you like words?
Words come out and play.
Words are free and words are friends
Words are great to say.

From The Day I Fell Down the Toilet and Other Poems
by Steve Turner

1   In pairs, think of examples of words for some of the lines in the above poem. For example, 'cheese' may be a word that makes you grin if photographers ask you to say it before they take your photo; 'holiday' may be a word that makes you glad; you might have just learned 'bonjour' in a French class.

2   In small groups, work on a performance of the poem in which two people read the original words, and others add their best words to illustrate the line. Make sure you use appropriate voices or actions for each of the lines to show their meaning. You might want to do it like this:

Voice 1 (smoothly):   **Words of love/That keep you warm,**
Voice 2:   'You're my wee pet'

Voice 3 (happily):   **Words that make you glad.**
Voice 4:   'Holidays are coming'

Voice 1 (sharply):   **Words that hit you, words that hurt,**
Voice 2:   'I hate you'

Voice 3 (sadly):   **Words that make you sad.**
Voice 4:   'It's all over'

When you have prepared it, perform it to another group or to the whole class.

Unit review

Here you will:

- review your own work
- recognise your strengths and weaknesses.

How well have you developed the following skills?

- Writing in the recount genre.
- Using strategies to improve spelling.
- Building up a portfolio of writing.
- Working with others in group discussion.
- Working with others in drama.
- Reading for understanding of others' early experiences.
- Comparing texts on a similar theme.

What else do you think you have learned? Discuss this in pairs, or small groups, or write your responses in your Writing Portfolio (see page 17).

Unit 2: Our environment

What we will be doing

In this unit we will:

- work individually, in pairs and in small groups
- investigate a range of text types relating to the environment
- use ICT (information and communications technology) to research and present a piece of written work about your local area.

What we will be learning

In this unit we will learn to:

- read a variety of texts with greater understanding
- recognise why a text is written (its purpose) and for whom (audience)
- write effectively in a range of forms.

Thinking skills and personal capabilities

In this unit we will:

- select the most appropriate information for a particular task
- select and classify text types
- compare and evaluate information
- show understanding of and communicate with a sense of audience and purpose
- use grids and charts to represent information.

Introduction

This unit is designed to help you to recognise some of the different types of texts you will be exploring in later units.

Recognising text types

  Task 1

In this task you will:

- read and discuss a range of texts
- confirm differences between fiction and non-fiction.

1   In pairs, look closely at the different types of text below.

2   Use a grid like this to divide them into **fiction** and **non-fiction**.

Fiction	Non-fiction

A The fish of Lough Neagh

The fresh waters of Lough Neagh and its river system provide a valuable habitat for many species of fish. Salmon, trout, eels, pollan, roach and bream feed on its abundant food supply which includes millions of Lough Neagh flies and their larvae, the bloodworms, which in turn feed on the rich supply of plant food in the Lough.

A special type of brown trout, known as the Dollaghan, is found in Lough Neagh and is thought to be unique to it. Similar to the more commonly found trout, this fish travels upstream during August and is found in all of the major rivers draining into Lough Neagh.

Pollan, sometimes known as the fresh water herring, is a uniquely Irish fish found only in Lough Neagh and a few other lakes. The fish spawn on the hard stony bottom found in some parts of the Lough.

Although Lough Neagh now supports a thriving commercial fishing industry as well as providing recreational angling, conservationists stress the dangers of overfishing in this area.

Adapted from The Resources of Lough Neagh *by Craigavon Borough Council.*

B

Last Tuesday, 10th October, our Year 8 Biology class set off from school in an Ulsterbus to Oxford Island.

We arrived in the car park at approximately 10.00am and, armed with clipboards, we set off in our designated groups to answer ten questions for our project.

First of all, my group went to the Woodland area and noted down the native trees, and numerous woodland flowers.

Next, we went to the waterside hide where we found bay tufted ducks and teal. We also managed to note some of the wild fowl around the lough shores before a thunder burst of rain. Then, because of the wet conditions, we were forced indoors.

Thankfully, in the afternoon, we were able to gain enough information from the audio-visual presentation in The Discovery Centre to finish our tasks.

C Country cooking

A Very Fishy Irish Stew

680g/1½lbs white cod (or firm white fish)
2dssp lemon juice
1tsp black peppercorns, ground
1dssp oil
30g/1oz butter or polyunsaturated fat
1 small bunch spring onions, cut into strips
2 leeks, cut into chunks
425ml/¾pt milk
1–2 bay leaves
2 carrots
115g/4oz white beans (canned)
70ml/⅛pt cream

TO GARNISH

2dssp parsley, finely chopped

Serves 6–8

Sprinkle the fish pieces with lemon juice and black pepper and leave to sit for several minutes. In a large pan heat the oil and butter then lightly cook the spring onion and pieces of leek. Add the fish pieces. Toss lightly for several minutes then add the milk, bay leaf, carrots and beans. Poach gently for 10–12 minutes until the fish is tender, but don't overcook. Just before serving remove the bay leaf, add cream if desired, garnish with parsley and serve.

From Jenny Bristow's Country Cooking 2

D Perch

Perched on their water perch hung in the clear Bann River
Near the clay bank in alder dapple and waver,

Perch they called 'grunts', little flood-slubs, runty and ready,
I saw and I see in the river's glorified body

That is passable through, but they're bluntly holding the pass,
Under the water-roof, over the bottom, adoze

On the current, against it, all muscle and slur
In the finland of perch, the fenland of alder, on air

That is water, on carpets of Bann Stream, on hold
In the everything flows and steady go of the world.

From Electric Light *by Seamus Heaney*

E Finn McCool

Finn was an Ulster tribal chieftain and commander of the King of Ireland's warriors. He was renowned in Ireland for his fighting ability and for his strength. What he could do is limited only by one's imagination! It was once said that Finn could pick thorns out of his heels while running.

Indeed once during a fight with a Scottish giant, he scooped up a huge clod of earth and flung it at his fleeing rival. The clod fell into the sea and turned into the Isle of Man. The hole it left filled up with water and became Lough Neagh, the largest lake in Ireland. All of these stories about Finn, and many more too, are certified as true according to the standards of Irish storytelling. For certain, he stands tall in the annals of Irish myth and legend.

F How is lignite formed?

Lignite is formed by the compression of plant materials into a solid form. Plant materials accumulate in water such as swamps, bogs or marshy areas. In these environments, there are minimal oxides so the plant material does not decay completely. Instead, bacteria partly decompose the oxygen and hydrogen in the organic material thus concentrating the carbon. The first product in the decomposition is peat. Then through the decay and burial of peat over a prolonged period of time, lignite is formed.

  ## Task 2

In this task you will:

- ask focused questions
- use your own ideas and ideas from others to inform decisions
- compare and evaluate information.

Look more closely at the examples of fiction and non-fiction texts in Extracts A–F.

1   In pairs, suggest some of the **differences** between the texts. For example, it is generally written in past tense/present tense, or it usually has a main character.

2   Outline these differences in a table like the one below.

Differences between fiction and non-fiction	
Fiction	Non-fiction

It helps when you read a text if you know:

- what kind of text it is
- why it was written (its purpose)
- who it was written for
- how it is constructed.

 Task 3

In this task you will:

- break the task into sub-tasks and select the most appropriate information for the task.

1   Look again at Extracts A–F and use a chart like the one below to clarify fiction or non-fiction, purpose, audience and genre.

Text	Fiction/Non-fiction	Purpose	Audience	Genre
A				
B				
C				
D				
E				
F				

2   If an extract is **non-fiction**, decide which of these **genres** fits most closely:

- **recount** – giving an account of what happened
- **report** – giving the reader facts about a subject
- **explanation** – giving reasons why or how something happened
- **exposition** – trying to influence the reader's behaviour
- **argument/discussion** – presenting both sides of the argument
- **procedure** – describing how something is done.

3   If an extract is **fiction**, decide which **genre** it belongs to, for example, romance, historical, myth or others.

4   Can you add any other examples of fictional genre?

Managing information

 Task 4

In this task you will:

- select and classify information.

Read through Extracts G and H which illustrate some of the differences between fiction and non-fiction writing.

- Extract G: description of Ardboe and surrounding area
- Extract H: description from a brochure about the Lough Neagh area.

G   All of Us There

Lower Ardboe lies along the shores of Lough Neagh, the biggest lake in the United Kingdom, twenty-five miles long by eight miles wide, in effect an inland tideless freshwater sea, an extravagant expanse of water which laps the small fields of our farm, within sight and sound of our house. Its soughing music forms the aural background to each day of our lives.

We are almost an island, connected to the outside world only by one tiny road which dribbles its slack and twisting way into our hidden demesnes, and which swerves and slings around the perimeter of the aerodrome like a girdle. To anyone coming towards us for the first time from the small market town of Cookstown ten miles away, following the road as it meanders towards the lough, it must appear to expire in a flaxhole and a tangle of bramble below the Moor Hill. But in fact, at that point, called the Cross Roads (although it is not strictly that), it turns at a right-angle, narrows and plunges towards Biddy's Brae, past our house and thence to the Old Cross of Ardboe, where it ends in the graveyard surrounding the Cross. Another smaller spur road called the Car Road branches off alongside the lough shore towards the flat long beauty of Golloman's Point, and parallel to that old turf road is a new white concrete road leading to the pump house built for a water supply to the aerodrome. Both these roads are hidden from view on the road to the Cross.

That road links us to our landscape in the same way that our sisterhood links us together. It is an absolute connection and has the quality of infinity as it stretches ahead in a green and blue haze. Along its way old men and sometimes an old woman lean over their gates or against a sagging gate-post made from the branch of a tree, waiting with an endless curiosity for our approach, as though they had never ever seen us before, nor even the likes of us, though they have known us from babyhood. They like to vex us with questions as to our goodness and badness, and what book we are in at school. In their day, when public elementary schooling was first established, each grade of student was reckoned according to which textbook she or he had attained and the form still lingers. We were always wary of the questioners and their questions and indeed they were asked to vex us, rather than from genuine interest, and sometimes adults did things that left us feeling helplessly violated; we were never sure why or when and thus we tended to be on guard.

From All of Us There *by Polly Devlin*

H   The fish of Lough Neagh

The fresh waters of Lough Neagh and its river system provide a valuable habitat for many species of fish. Trout, salmon, eels, pollan, perch, roach and bream feed on the abundant food supply which includes millions of Lough Neagh Flies and their larvae, the bloodworms, which in turn feed on the rich supply of plant food in the Lough.

A special type of brown trout, known as the Dollaghan, is found in Lough Neagh and is thought to be unique to it. Similar to the more commonly found trout, this fish travels upstream during August and is found in all of the major rivers draining into Lough Neagh. Dollaghan spawn in the gravel beds of the rivers at the end of October and then return to the Lough.

Pike are a predatory fish, living on a diet of smaller fishes, insects and aquatic invertebrates. Their large heads and powerful jaws enable them to hunt efficiently. They lie motionless in water, or lurk in clumps of weeds and then move swiftly to catch their prey. They spawn in weedy shallows from late winter to early spring.

Bream are found throughout Lough Neagh and in some of the surrounding lakes. They live in shallow water where there is a muddy bottom and spawn from mid April to mid May, preferring areas where there are rushes and reeds.

Bream are fished mainly in the winter and can be easily caught in nets as they feed in large schools along the bottom though they are of little commercial value.

Pollan, sometimes known as the fresh water herring, is a uniquely Irish fish found only in Lough Neagh and a few other lakes. Shoals of pollan spend their life in the fresh waters of the Lough feeding on Chironomid larvae (bloodworms), perch fry, fresh water snails and their eggs and plankton. The fish spawn on the hard stony or gravely bottom found in some parts of the Lough. When they are mature they always move in shoals.

The Lough supports a thriving commercial fishing industry as well as providing recreational angling. Commercial fishing in the Lough on a large scale is relatively recent in comparison to the thousands of years in which fishing has been carried out. This century, however, pollution, powered fishing craft and the adoption of sophisticated netting systems has led to a dramatic decline in fish populations, particularly of pollan and trout. Today stocks are managed by the Fisheries Conservancy Board of the Department of the Environment who sells licences, regulates net sizes, sets fishing season dates, prevents poaching and monitors pollution.

Adapted from The Resources of Lough Neagh *by Craigavon Borough Council.*

1 What do you notice?

2 Indicate some of the **differences** in a chart like this one.

	Area around Ardboe	Lough Neagh area
Fiction/Non-fiction		
Structure/Layout/ Length of sentences		
Verbs		
Adjectives		

3 Look closely at the verbs in paragraph 2 in Extract G (Ardboe) and compare these to the verbs used in Extract H (the description of Lough Neagh).

• Comment specifically on the use of the verbs: *dribbles*, *swerves*, *slings*.

• What is the main difference between these and the verbs used in the report on Lough Neagh?

Task 5

In this task you will:

- use your own and others' ideas to locate information and select the most appropriate information for the task

- be a text detective.

1   Explore a number of non-fiction texts in more detail.

2   Try to find an example of typical **features** of this text type.

3   Include this sheet in your Writing Portfolio for later discussions.

Extension task: Thinking

1   Which would be the best **text type** or **genre** to use to give a dramatic account of a recent ski trip?

2   Which **text type/genre** would you use to give exact instructions on how to build a DIY wardrobe?

3   Which **text type/genre** would provide you with the most information if you wanted to find out about wildlife around Lough Neagh?

Task 6

In this task you will:

- compare and evaluate information
- make decisions based on purpose and audience.

Once you know what it is that you are trying to do **(purpose)**, then you can choose an appropriate **form** to communicate your thoughts.

1   In pairs, decide which **form** (format) you might use for the purposes below.

2   In pairs, try to think of two or three examples for each purpose and form. Then make a group of four or five and share your ideas.

Purpose	Form
To record feelings, emotions, observations	(e.g. letter)
To persuade To amuse or entertain To command or direct	(e.g. speech)

Remember, before doing a piece of writing always ask:

- What is the **purpose**? Who is the **audience**?
- What is the **genre** or **text type**?
- What is the best **form** to use?

Writing a non-chronological report

   Task 7

In this task you will:

- plan a report
- break a task into sub-tasks
- research and select the most appropriate information for the task
- communicate with a sense of audience and purpose.

Read a report, for example Extract A in Task 1 on fish in Lough Neagh.

1   Consider how a report is written.
2   What happens in the opening paragraph?
3   What purpose has the final paragraph?

Independent writing activity

1   Write a report about your local area.
2   Look back to the features of non-fiction which you outlined in your grid.
3   Research your area using ICT or use local information packs.
4   Write at least five paragraphs of your own.
5   Try to include diagrams, photographs or pictures to support your report.

Unit review

Here you will:

- review the work of this unit
- consider what you have learned about genre and form.

Discuss the following questions in pairs, or write responses in your Writing Portfolio:

- What is the main difference between fiction and non-fiction texts?
- What are the main fiction genres?
- What are the main non-fiction genres?
- What are the main **forms** of writing within non-fiction genre?
- What are the four aspects you should consider before doing a piece of writing?

Unit 3: Rhyme and reason

What we will be doing

In this unit we will:

- read a range of poems
- write your own poems
- talk about the poems you read and write
- work in groups on a dramatic presentation of a poem
- record a reading of a poem using sound effects
- add to your Writing Portfolio.

What we will be learning

In this unit we will:

- develop personal tastes and preferences
- plan the writing process
- understand the differences between a range of poetic forms
- review your own and others' writing.

Thinking skills and personal capabilities

In this unit we will:

- learn from and build on your own and others' ideas and experiences
- use all of the senses to stimulate and contribute to ideas
- work with others as part of a group
- value other people's ideas.

What is poetry?

 ## Task 1

In this task you will:

- reflect upon and discuss your experiences of poetry.

1 Can you remember any of the poems you read in primary school? Are there any you liked in particular?

2 How did you study poetry? Did you read it to yourself or out loud? Perhaps you performed poems in groups or as a whole class, adding movement and music?

3 What type of poems did you write? Did you find it enjoyable or difficult?

4 Is poetry different from other types of writing?

5 What is special or unique about poetry?

 ## Task 2

In this task you will:

- read a range of different text types
- decide in pairs which are poems.

1 Read the extracts below. Decide which texts are poems and which are not.

1

Come away, O human child! To the waters and the wild with a faery, hand in hand, for the world's more full of weeping than you can understand.

2

So unchanging was the dull old house, the yellow light in the darkened room, the faded spectre in the chair by the dressing-table glass …

3

This is just to say I have eaten the plums that were in the icebox and which you were probably saving for breakfast. Forgive me they were delicious so sweet and so cold.

4

Birthdays are a chance to say how much I love you every day. But once a year it comes the time to say I'm glad that you are mine.

2 How did you decide whether the examples are poems or not?

3 In groups of four, make a list of features which you believe to be the ingredients of a poem.

4 Present and display the agreed features of poetry on a class poster.

Limericks

One of the things you may have mentioned when putting together your list of features of a poem is that a poem should rhyme. Read the following poems which have a very definite rhyme scheme.

An elderly lady from Fleet
Once scored a goal with both feet,
And despite her great age,
Earns a reasonable wage
As reserve centre forward for Crete.

From Limericks *by Michael Palin*

A flea and a fly in a flue
Were imprisoned, so what could they do?
Said the fly, 'Let us flee!'
'Let us fly!' said the flea.
So they flew through a flaw in the flue.

Anon

A curious young man from Calcutta,
Was known as a bit of a nutter.
After prawn vindaloo
And a Guinness or two
He'd lie very still in the gutter.

From Limericks *by Michael Palin*

This type of poem is called a **limerick**. It has a particular pattern and rhythm.

Task 3

In this task you will:

- consider the features of a limerick.

In pairs, try to work out the main features of limericks, for example:

- rhyming pattern
- number of beats per line
- number of lines
- anything else that you may notice.

Homophones are words that sound the same but have different spellings and meanings. For example:

- eight/ate
- flour/flower
- allowed/aloud.

 Task 4

In this task you will:

- discuss homophones and why poets use them.

1   Can you think of other homophones?
2   Work in pairs to find examples of homophones in the limericks.
3   Why would a poet use homophones?
4   Why would a poet select the limerick form?

Task 5

In this task you will:

* write your own limerick.

Now it is your turn to write a limerick. Below are some first lines to help you get started.

* *There once was a girl called Clare …*
* *A giraffe called Jim from Tyrone …*
* *A silly young man from Belfast …*
* *There was a strange dog from Ardglass …*

Evaluation

  Task 6

In this task you will:

* reflect on your writing.

Having shared your limericks with others, reflect on what you have achieved. Consider the following questions and reflect on them in your Writing Portfolio.

1   Was it easy to come up with rhymes for your word choices?
2   How did you think of rhyming words? What tips would you pass on to the rest of the class? How does your limerick fit the pattern of limericks? Did you use homophones?
3   Does your limerick make sense? Do limericks have to make sense?

Haiku

Haiku is a Japanese form of poetry. Before we look at the pattern of the haiku, remind yourself of what a **syllable** is.

Discuss the following in pairs.

1   How many syllables are there in your name? (Tap out the beats.)
2   Think of three words that have only one syllable.
3   Which months of the year have four syllables?

Task 7

In this task you will:

- read and decide on the main features of a haiku.

1 Read the following examples of haiku. Work in pairs to decide on the main features of a haiku.

2 Make a list and share your decisions with another pair.

My mum declares peace.
She hands out bouquets of flowers.
Laughter like church bells.

> *By Pie Corbett, from* Rice, Pie and Moses *by
> John Rice, Pie Corbett and Brian Moses*

Curving up, then down.
Meeting blue sky and green earth
Melding sun and rain.

> *Donna Brock*

Exploring the world
And yet never far from home:
Snail crosses my path.

> *Philip Adams*

 Task 8

In this task you will:

- write your own haiku.

Haiku are like snapshots of a particular moment fixed in time.

1 Choose an image. It can be from your own photo collection or from a book or magazine.

2 Use this image to help you write your own haiku.

Evaluation

Consider the following questions and reflect on them in your Writing Portfolio:

1   Is your finished poem a haiku? How do you know?
2   What did you enjoy about writing this poem?
3   What was the most difficult thing about writing your haiku?

Sense poems

One of the techniques poets use is to appeal to our senses. What are our five senses? Which of your senses do you consider to be the most important? Defend your choice.

 Task 9

In this task you will:

•   discuss your ideas in pairs.

Discuss with a partner:

1   Do smells remind you of a certain person, place or time?
2   What smells remind you of Christmas, Hallowe'en or primary school?
3   Can you think of any other places or people that have distinctive smells?

Task 10

In this task you will:

- work on a group presentation of a poem.

Read the following poem in a small group. Share out the lines among members of the group and do a presentation for the whole class:

Sunday smells of bacon and eggs

Sunday smells of bacon and eggs
And hot, baked lazing cars.
Monday smells of washing
And fresh air.
Tuesday smells of less activity,
Of ironing, tea and biscuits.
Wednesday smells lonely, bleak,
Stuck there – mid of the week –
Supported by a rhyme.
Thursday is sturdier,
Smells of rich beef stew
With dumplings, we hope.
Friday smells of week-old-bed-clothes
Weaving me into the body of the bed
In dowsing, rotting doze;
Yes, Friday smellz!
Splendid Saturday
Smells of shortbread, fairy cakes,
Sausages and onions,
Apple-crumble and not school custard.
Sunday again –
And Sunday ought to smell of church
Dead mice and incense.
Sorry, but no.
It smells of ragged curtains
For home made camps
And battered old bikes,
And Friends.

Jill Campbell

Task 11

In this task you will:

- read a poem for understanding.

What do you learn about the poet and her life from the poem above? To answer this question, copy and complete the table below.

The poet's life	Details	Evidence from the poem: How do you know?
The poet's age		
Her home		
Poet's likes		
Poet's dislikes		

 ## Task 12

In this task you will:

- write your own sense poem.

Write your own poem entitled 'Sunday smells of …' Follow the format of Jill Campbell's poem and **make sure** that you are creating a sense poem.

Sounds

  Task 13

In this task you will:

- be aware of sounds in the environment
- read a poem about and discuss the sense of hearing.

Time yourself for one minute. In this time, your classmates and you should be completely silent. Listen very carefully to all the sounds in the classroom. After the minute, make a note of all the sounds you heard. Is there such a thing as the sound of silence?

In a Moment of Silence

In a moment of silence, I heard my Mum bump out of bed.
I heard her dawdle downstairs.
I heard her creak into the kitchen.

In a moment of silence, I heard the radio rabbiting to her.
I heard our budgie babbling to her.
I heard the kettle calling to her.

In a moment of silence I heard clattering cups.
I heard breakfast bowls.
I heard stainless steel spoons.

In a moment of silence, I heard my stomach rumble –
so I got up for something to eat!

Michael Coleman

 Task 14

In this task you will:

- explore sound and its impact and meaning in poetry.

1   Make a list of the different sounds the poet hears in the above poem.
2   Choose three words from the poem that are used to describe the sounds being made.
3   Can you think of three other words used to describe sounds?
4   Find words to describe the sounds made by the following:
    - a baby
    - saucepans
    - a chainsaw
    - a frog.

5   **Onomatopoeia** is when a word sounds like the thing it describes, for example, *hiss*, *slap*, *bang*. Can you think of others?

Task 15

In this task you will:

- perform a dramatic reading of a poem using sound effects.

In small groups, prepare a dramatic reading of the sense poem, which you wrote for Task 12, for a radio programme about poetry. Your reading should include as many sound effects from the poem as possible. As a group, decide how to produce these sound effects.

Simile and metaphor

 ## Task 16

In this task you will:

- come up with a definition for a simile and a metaphor.

Poets use certain poetic effects to create images and meaning for the reader.

1   Read the sentences below and work out (in pairs) a definition for a **simile** and a **metaphor**.

    a   (Simile) His face was as white as a sheet.

    b   (Simile) The sky blazed like a bubbling cauldron.

    c   (Metaphor) The sea is an angry dog.

    d   (Metaphor) They sailed out of the mouth of the river.

2   Agree definitions and share with another pair.

3   Present agreed definitions to the rest of the class.

Task 17

In this task you will:

- examine the effects of comparison.

Answer these questions about the following poem.

1 Why are the snake's eyes compared to raisins?
2 What type of comparison is this?
3 What are her fangs like?
4 What kind of comparison is this?
5 How is the snake like a lasso?
6 What two things are used to suggest the movements of the snake's body?
7 The poem creates a strong mental image of a snake. Choose one image from the poem which you think best describes the snake.

Diamond Rattlesnake

Her tough skin glistens
in the burning sunlight.
Dark raisin eyes sparkle –
fangs like curved icicles.

She traces an S in the sand
leaving picture patterns.
A writhing, slithering lasso
on her slow journey to wherever.

Arching like a gymnast,
curving like a living rainbow,
no instrument can match her music.

By John Rice, from Rice, Pie and Moses *by
John Rice, Pie Corbett and Brian Moses*

Task 18

In this task you will:

- write a descriptive poem.

1 Look closely at a picture or image of an animal or object.
2 Write down any word or phrases that come to mind when you see it.
3 Think of two similes and two metaphors that can be used to describe it.
4 Now use these words, phrases, similes and metaphors to write a descriptive poem.

  Task 19

In this task you will:

- write imaginatively based on your reading of an image
- explore senses and feelings.

Examine the picture in Task 18 and answer the following questions.

1 What time of year is it? What time of day?
2 What is happening in the picture?
3 What sounds would you hear if you were there? Choose interesting words to describe these sounds.
4 Is there anything in the picture that you would like to touch? What would it feel like?
5 What would you smell if you were there?
6 How would you feel if you were in this picture? Explain your feelings.
7 Think of a simile or metaphor you could use to describe what you see.

Task 20

In this task you will:

- write your own sense poem.

Write a poem describing the place you see in the picture in Task 18. Make use of the knowledge you have already gained in this unit about poetry.

Unit review

Here you will:

- review what you now know about forms of poetry.

Write your responses to the following in your Writing Portfolio:

- What have you learned about poetic forms?
- What do you now know about poetic language in this unit?
- Do you like working with others? Does it improve your learning? How does it help?
- What else did you discover in this unit?

Unit 4: The reader's point of view

What we will be doing

In this unit we will:

- work individually, in pairs and in groups
- make an oral presentation
- write a piece of fiction from a particular viewpoint
- record thoughts in the Writing Portfolio.

What we will be learning

In this unit we will learn to:

- recognise the viewpoint from which a text is written and to express empathy
- understand first, second and third person
- classify and order sets of words to identify shades of meaning
- understand how language affects our attitude to text
- use language with precision and for effect
- use a thesaurus and understand its function.

Thinking skills and personal capabilities

In this unit we will:

- avoid jumping to conclusions
- make decisions, offer solutions and take action based on knowledge
- weigh up pros and cons of different opinions
- understand more than one point of view
- examine options and weigh up pros and cons
- try alternative approaches
- use different kinds of questions systematically and with purpose.

Seeing things

  Task 1

In this task you will:

- weigh up pros and cons of different opinions
- describe or depict ideas in ways that can be understood by others.

The Blind Men and the Elephant

It was six men of Hindostan,
To learning much inclined,
Who went to see the Elephant
(Though all of them were blind);
That each by observation
Might satisfy his mind.

The First approached the Elephant
And happening to fall
Against his broad and sturdy side,
At once began to bawl:
'Bless me, it seems the Elephant
Is very like a wall.'

The Second, feeling of his tusk,
Cried, 'Ho! What have we here
So very round and smooth and sharp?
To me 'tis mighty clear
This marvel of an Elephant
Is very like a spear.'

The Third approached the animal,
And happening to take
The squirming trunk within his hands,
Then boldly up and spake:
'I see,' quoth he, 'the Elephant
Is very like a snake.'

The Fourth stretched out his eager hand
And felt about the knee,
'What most this mighty beast is like
Is mighty plain,' quoth he;
''Tis clear enough the Elephant
Is very like a tree.'

The Fifth who chanced to touch the ear
Said: 'Even the blindest man
Can tell what this resembles most;
Deny the fact who can,
This marvel of an Elephant
Is very like a fan.'

The Sixth no sooner had begun
About the beast to grope
Than, seizing on the swinging tail
That fell within his scope,
'I see,' quoth he, 'the Elephant
Is very like a rope.'

And so these men of Hindostan
Disputed loud and long,
Each of his own opinion
Exceeding stiff and strong,
Though each was partly in the right,
And all were in the wrong.

John Godfrey Saxe

1   In pairs, **list** the six things the blind men thought the elephant was.

2   What does the poet mean when he says the following?

'Though each was partly in the right,

And all were in the wrong.'

3   Does it matter how we approach things?

Task 2

In this task you will:

- work with others
- take personal responsibility for assigned work
- work in teams
- predict consequences of actions
- investigate how an incident can be seen in different ways.

Look at these pictures. In groups, **discuss** what is happening in them.

1. Why was Tiny Tim sent to the headmaster?

2. Did Jonty behave fairly?

3. Form a group and assign a **role** to each member of the group: Tiny Tim, Orca, Jonty, headmaster, secretary, any witnesses to the scene in the playground. Let each person give a version of the incident as he or she sees it.

4. What do you think **point of view** means?

 Task 3

In this task you will:

- see value in considering other viewpoints
- avoid jumping to conclusions.

Read the following extracts from a novel that tells the story of Cindy and Ashling and their parents. It is written in diary form, with Cindy's diary entries composing one half of the book, and Ashling's the other half. Ashling and her sister, Alva, live with their divorced mother, Margaret. Cindy lives with her widowed father, Richard. Margaret and Richard have struck up a friendship. This is the first time the girls meet.

Diaries are written in the **first person**. As you read these extracts consider what effect this has on the writer and on the reader.

> **Glossary**
>
> First person – I, we
> Second person – you
> Third person – he, she, it, they

Sisters . . . No Way!

Cindy's diary: Sunday 29th June

I don't know where to begin. The menu, maybe, as that's the simplest part. He did his famous roast lamb with rosemary and garlic, with all the trimmings, mint sauce, redcurrant jelly, roast spuds, glazed parsnips, petit pois (frozen, of course), and to give him his due it was absolutely delicious. He served a nice Australian Cabernet Sauvignon with it, but that's another story. No starter. He says it's not traditional for Sunday lunch. The younger Magees thought the Baked Alaska was scrum, even though it wasn't quite a success – I don't think the oven was hot enough. They are that sort of family. People who use words like 'scrum'. Can you imagine? They wore *kilts*, one in greens and one in blues. They looked like two little girls dressed up to go out to Sunday lunch, which is what they

were, except they aren't little. I bet their mother had them in matching clothes when they were smaller. You know, two little tartan dresses from Laura Ashley, and two matching velvet headbands. They were, as you will have gathered from this description, unspeakable. Oh yes, and they both had little pearl stud earrings, just like their mother's. No wonder the father bailed out. Between Miss Prim and Miss Proper and the Bay tree he must have had a dog's life.

I wore jeans and a HMV sweatshirt, and I alternated between feeling really cool and hip and, well, normal, and feeling sort of coarse and out of place in this genteel gathering. I have to admit that I drank too much wine. Dad is pretty laid back about alcohol. I think he has this theory that if children drink at home and with parental approval they are less likely to drink because of peer pressure and so to abuse alcohol. I agree with that theory, actually, and I think I am a shining example of its soundness most of the time. I have the odd glass of wine on a Sunday with my dad and that's as far as it goes – usually.

But this Sunday was a bit different. I had my usual glass of wine – Ashling, who is sixteen, was allowed a quarter glass topped up with water, why bother? I thought, it might as well be Ribena at that dilution – and then I snuck another glass, more out of boredom, really, than anything else. After that, I just kept pouring. Nobody noticed. Well, precisely. I might as well not have been there, as far as the lovebirds were concerned, and as for Little Miss Moffat and Miss Goody Two-Shoes, they were too busy wiping their mouths carefully with their napkins and saying please and thank you and would you ever pass the butter. They said nothing else throughout the meal, just chewed with great concentration.

For all they looked like a picture out of a Marks and Spencer catalogue, they hadn't a clue really how to behave. Please and thank you and using your napkin are all very well, but true courtesy involves making the other person feel less uncomfortable. They don't know the first thing about true courtesy.

So I just sipped away quietly at the Cabernet Sauvignon, and after a bit a sort of a rosy glow descended and I stopped caring about being the only unpartnered person in the room. I probably talked a bit much. I usually do, after a glass of wine, but I don't think I said anything shameful. I certainly felt rather warm about the cheeks, and I may have been a bit on the waspish side about the Baked Alaska, I can't be sure. But I know I didn't do or say anything outrageous. I know that at one point I told Margaret all the teachers' nicknames. She didn't understand most of them, including her own.

What has my life come to, that I should spend a Sunday afternoon like this?

Ashling's diary: Sunday 29th June

It turns out her name is Cindy. It's all right for a doll or a supermodel, but a real girl called Cindy! She certainly doesn't look like a supermodel. She wore a T-shirt that looked as if she'd slept in it and awful jeans. Not only had they tears in them, I think they were actually dirty.

And the food was delicious too, proper Sunday food. Lamb I think we had. Richard cooked it himself. He is quite proud of his cooking. You'd expect somebody interested in food to be fatter.

He fussed around with chafing dishes and chargers – I never even heard of these things until I heard him talking about them – at a great rate, but Cindy just sat there and looked bored. She hardly said a word through the meal. I thought at first maybe she was shy, and I tried to say a few things to her, but she didn't pick up any of my conversational openings, so Alva and I ended up just saying things like pass the butter. We were trying very hard, for Mum's sake.

Her dad produced a bottle of red wine. He's really a very nice man. Or seems to be. He offered me some. I had a little drop, but I don't really drink, so I topped it up with water. I think that was a mistake, because it tasted terrible. Alva got Coke, and I was sorry I hadn't asked for some too. But Cindy really lashed into the wine, and after her third glass she was jabbering away about nothing in particular, mostly schoolfriends of hers, particularly somebody called Lisa, which were of no interest to us. I think Mum quite enjoyed some of it because she knew the people she was talking about, from school. She talked about the teachers a bit as well, and told Mum what their nicknames were. They weren't very original. And she was rude about the food. Alva said the dessert was scrumptious, and she looked witheringly at her and said it was scum, not scrum.

It wasn't my idea of a great way to spend a Sunday afternoon.

Extract from Sisters . . . No Way! *by Siobhán Parkinson*

Answer the following questions:

Note

The ability to identify with another person and to understand fully what they are feeling or thinking is called **empathy**

1   Why do you think the author, Siobhán Parkinson, chose to construct the novel like this?

2   Is one version of the events right and the other wrong?

3   Can you understand how either of the girls is feeling?

4   Describe, in writing, the same incident from either the mother's or the father's viewpoint.

Task 4

In this task you will:

- work with others
- generate and group ideas.

Read these two extracts from *Shadow of the Beast* by Maggie Pearson.

Troy has been unwell and has gone to live with his foster parents while he waits for his father to come for him. Sometimes he feels lonely and he spends a great deal of time walking and cycling around the countryside.

Shadow of the Beast (extract 1)

There were no elms any more in the village of Elm Green, not since the Dutch elm disease. The 'green' had never been more than a muddy hump, worn bare of grass by people stamping their feet warm while they waited for the one bus out per day. A scatter of tumbledown cottages, two squat, grey Victorian terraces and a red-brick council estate with pebbledash bungalows for the old folk. One church, St Edmund's, not specially old or interesting. One pub, The New Inn, ditto. One post office cum general store. That was Elm Green.

He kept on walking till he was out of the village and on towards the sea, still walking, past the ploughed field … one field of soggy sheep … one threadbare meadow. After that there was nothing but rough scrub, stunted bushes and clumps of skeleton blades of grass whispering together. The road dwindled to a dirt track sloping upwards, soft soil dragging at his feet. By the time he reached the top his legs were so weary he just let them fold under him and sat with a thump on the damp, greyish sand.

In front of him the beach swept down more gently than the slope he'd climbed. The grass grew more spare, half buried in drifting sand, till the sand became shingle, sloping to the water's edge, white-toothed wavelets nibbling at the edges of the land. Coastal erosion. Awesome. Chances were that in a hundred years all this bit of coastline would be gone. In two hundred the village itself, maybe. Nothing left but the sea.

From Shadow of the Beast *by Maggie Pearson*

Shadow of the Beast (extract 2)

They drove through empty, lamplit, rain-washed streets, the houses drifting further apart as they came to the suburbs. Clipped suburban hedges gave way to wild tangles of hawthorn and briars and bare trees stark against the velvet sky.

Through the rain-streaked window, Troy caught flashes of movement – night creatures prowling in the shadows, a dog, a cat, a fox. Nothing to be afraid of. Now and again they met a car or a lorry. Once they passed a man on a bike. Mostly they had the road to themselves.

Lulled by the click-click of the windscreen wipers swinging back and forth, Troy dozed. When he woke again the rain had stopped. The moon and the stars were out. The van was purring through the sleeping countryside, wheels swishing through the puddles. Past dreaming cottages, smoke whispering from the chimneys in the moonlight. The road was a ribbon of light spinning itself out of the darkness. Rabbits on the verges snapped to attention, noses twitching, in the glare of the headlamps. A pale owl swooped low across the road in front of them.

As they crested the hill and came within sight of the village, a pearly light was spreading across the eastern sky. It was not dawn yet, but the day would come.

From Shadow of the Beast *by Maggie Pearson*

In **pairs** discuss the answers to these questions.

1   Is Troy comfortable in extract 1?

2   Is Troy comfortable in extract 2?

3   Some words used in these extracts are not merely descriptive, but
     emotive – they help us understand Troy's emotions at the time. List the
     words you consider to be emotive.

4   Move into groups of four and compare your lists. What **effect** do these
     words have on you?

5   Could you change some of these words to others which would change
     our impression of Troy's feelings?

6   Some writers **use words carefully** to ensure their readers think, feel or
     act in a particular way. They select words that are just right. **Emotive
     words** can be important here, and the writer sometimes has to select
     from words that mean almost the same thing, but have different **shades
     of meaning**.

For example: **surprising, remarkable, wonderful, amazing, awesome**
are all words which express a reaction to something that affects you deeply.
They have been arranged from the **gentlest to the strongest**.

Try to find words that have similar meanings to a given word. Arrange them
in the same fashion in the table your teacher gives you.

Task 5

In this task you will:

- select and integrate information from different sources
- make new connections between ideas/information.

Just as a writer has a **choice of words** at his or her disposal, he or she also has a **choice of narrators**. In fiction, the person telling the story is the **narrator**.

A writer can use one of several **narrating voices** depending on what he or she wants the reader to know, think or feel. He or she can choose from:

First person narrator	Third person narrator	Omniscient narrator
The first person narrator is a character in a story who relates the events as he or she sees them. The first person narrator can also express his or her **own** thoughts and feelings. This narrator uses the first person saying, 'I did …'; 'I saw …'; 'I felt…'. We can usually **empathise** with this person.	The writer can use the third person – he, she, they – so that we see the events through the eyes of **one specific character**. We know what this person is thinking and feeling, and of events and other characters from his or her observations. We may not be given enough information to fully **empathise** with the other characters.	This is when the narrator is not one character in the story, but is **omniscient** and reveals not only the actions but also the thoughts and feelings of all the characters in the story. The writer uses the third person – he, she, they.

Read an extract from a novel. In pairs, discuss your extracts, and answer the following questions.

1   Which **narrating voice** is the writer using in each of the extracts?

2   What **effect** does this have on you?

3   Why do you think the writer chooses a particular viewpoint?

4   If a story is told from one viewpoint only, are there any **advantages** for the reader?

5   If a story has only one viewpoint, what does a reader need to be aware of?

6   Does an **omniscient narrator** make a story more or less interesting?

Task 6

In this task you will:

- work with others
- take time to be imaginative
- engage and persevere with the task.

Brainstorm all the traditional tales you know, such as *Babes in the Wood*, *Goldilocks and the Three Bears*, etc.

1   Which **narrating voice** is normally used in the telling of these tales?

2   Select a traditional tale. In pairs, discuss your chosen tales. Identify the narrator's voice.

3   Choose a different character from within the tale. Tell the story from that character's point of view. Discuss this interpretation of the story and how your attitude to the characters or events was disturbed or changed.

4   Write your version of the story.

5   Read your tale to the class.

Unit review

Here you will:

- review your own work
- recognise your personal strengths and weaknesses.

Discuss the following in pairs or small groups and record your responses in your Writing Portfolio:

- What do you understand by 'point of view'?
- What is the effect of using first, second or third person?
- What is the effect of emotive language?
- How can empathy be aroused?
- What do you know about the use of a thesaurus?
- What else do you think you have learned?

In this unit you have had practice in problem solving and thinking creatively.

- Re-read your Writing Portfolio and decide in which skill you feel you are strong and on which you may need to work.

You have been discussing the ways in which writers use **words to influence** their readers and how it is possible to **identify a point of view** in writing. Think back to the start of this unit.

- Has your viewpoint of writers changed? How?
- Select and share with others in a group a short piece of writing written from a particular viewpoint.

Unit 5: Reader's Theatre

What we will be doing

In this unit we will:

- present a Reader's Theatre performance
- understand the layout, organisation and language of a drama text
- review words and phrases associated with drama text and performance
- check basic punctuation rules connected to drama texts
- experiment with adverbs as part of speech tags.

What we will be learning

In this unit we will learn to:

- read and adapt texts for performance as a Reader's Theatre
- work in small groups to think and plan.

Thinking skills and personal capabilities

In this unit we will:

- take responsibility for tasks and roles in a group
- work to reach agreement in groups
- adapt behaviour and language to suit audience and purpose
- critically evaluate ideas.

Introduction

Reader's Theatre is a term that refers to the use or creation of scripts for a special kind of reading performance. It is different from drama because you do not need to learn lines, have costumes or complicated stage sets. What you do is try to make meaning and explore texts mainly by using your voice. It is fun but it can also present challenges. It should encourage you to ask questions and engage in plenty of discussion.

What is involved?

You will need to:

- choose or write a script (sources for scripts can be stories, history, arguments, non-fiction, newspaper reports and so on)
- establish roles in small groups: director, narrator, characters
- read and re-read the text in order to consider alternative meanings for it
- practise the reading
- find a performance space
- give every reader a music stand for the scripts
- decide on any props or simple costuming that are needed
- agree on positioning
- block out or plan the performance
- explore meaning and become aware of different opinions and interpretations.

Preparing for Reader's Theatre

Oral interpretation
In Reader's Theatre, it is important to experiment with words and sentences to discover the many meanings that could be taken from them.

 ## Task 1

In this task you will:

- work together
- share ideas.

Experiment with the following sentence:

> 'Your form teacher wants to see you now.'

1   Work in small groups and repeat the sentence, **emphasising** a different word each time. Discuss how you think the meaning changed. Why did the meaning change?

2   Choose a sentence of your own in your group and experiment with creating different meanings. Did the meaning change?

Task 2

In this task you will:

- discuss how listeners pick up clues to meaning.

Scripts often tell the reader how to say the lines. A word may appear before the line, for example:

> Tom (apologetically), 'I'm sorry. I forgot all about our meeting.'
>
> John (angrily), 'Because of your bad memory we lost the contract.'

1   In pairs, take turns to read the sentences below to one another, using the adverbs *in italics* to help you express the emotion.

> (*Timidly*) 'Please don't ask me. I never know the right answer.'
>
> (*Angrily*) 'Put that away! I will not tell you again!'
>
> (*Sadly*) 'We will miss you when you have gone.'
>
> (*Stubbornly*) 'Why should I clean my room? Nobody in my class ever cleans their room!'
>
> (*Guiltily*) 'It definitely wasn't me. I was nowhere near the goal when the ball went in.'

2   In pairs, switch the **adverbs** around and note the effect on the sentences.

Task 3

In this task you will:

- collect adverbs and adverb phrases.

1   In small groups, collate a word bank of effective adverbs (*excitedly*) or adverb phrases (*in amazement*) that would help a reader to understand how a character is feeling or reacting.

2   Display the word banks in the classroom.

Other clues to interpreting meaning

3   Discuss with a partner what other clues may be available to a reader to help understand what is happening in a text.

  Task 4

In this task you will:

- work in small groups
- explore how meanings are made.

Work in groups of three: show awareness of differences of opinion.

1   Think of a simple sentence, for example:

> How long will you be?
>
> I am sorry about it.
>
> Don't come to this house again.

2   Decide on a situation or context for the scene, for example: Where is it happening? Who is present? What is the situation?

3   Choose an adverb or adverb phrase from your word bank.

4   Practise reading your sentence, and then read it to the class, using all the vocal clues.

5   The class may guess what is happening in the scene.

Reading between the lines

A sentence may have one meaning on the surface and other meanings beneath the surface. For example the following sentence, 'I wish I could do that', could mean:

- I'm envious of your great golf swing.
- You are ignoring my obvious handicap.
- I could probably do it much better, given the chance.
- Is there any way you could help me to do it?

 Task 5

In this task you will:

- discuss the effects of emphasis and tone in oral communication.

Think of two or three other meanings for each of the following sentences. Try to justify your opinions.

> 'Where are you going?'
>
> 'I love swimming.'
>
> 'Is this yours?'
>
> 'I wish I had the time.'

Body language

The way we use non-verbal language can communicate emotions and attitudes, often as effectively as words. Consider what might be meant by body language.

 Task 6

In this task you will:

- demonstrate the effects of body language.

1   In pairs, demonstrate an emotion such as: **anger**, **surprise**, **sadness**, **regret** to your partner, without using words.

2   In pairs, choose any one of the sentences below and express it to your partner, using only body language:

- 'It's very warm in here.'
- 'Don't come near me!'
- 'This is so boring.'
- 'What do you mean?'
- 'Please let me help.'
- 'Come in.'
- 'Go away!'
- 'You cannot mean it.'

3   Discuss as a class how you felt when expressing the body language.

4   Make a list of the most common body language signals.

5   Create more sentences and act them out. Comment on each other's interpretations and make suggestions for changes and improvements.

Time to do Reader's Theatre

Reading and staging a text

Task 7

In this task you will:

- work together
- impose meaning on a text.

On the next page is a text that can be used for a Reader's Theatre performance.

1 Read and discuss the text in small groups.

2 Mark and code the text for characters.

3 Identify readers for each character:

Cast

Chief Tiger (CT)

Lady (L)

Tigers 2 or 3 (T2 T3)

Narrator 1 (N1)

Narrator 2 (N2).

4 Assign roles in your group.

5 Do not change the text, but it can be effective to add sound effects, for example, growls, screams, etc.

6 Read through the text.

7 Rehearse reading, paying attention to character and expression.

8 When reading, arrange music stands, either:

- simply in a straight line

or:

- main characters or narrators located downstage centre; less important characters stage right and stage left

or:

- be creative and decide on your own positioning.

9 After the performance, discuss its impact.

Group evaluation

The best part was …

The part we could have improved was …

One problem we had was …

We solved it by …

Ladies First

Did you hear the one about the little girl who was a tender, sweet young thing?

Well, that's the way she thought of herself.

And this tender, sweet young thing spent a great deal of time just looking in the mirror and saying: [*indicating each item by pointing*]

'I am a real little lady. Anybody could tell that.

I wear lovely starched cotton dresses with matching ribbons in my lovely curly locks.

I wear clean white socks and shiny black patent leather shoes, and I always put just a dab of perfume behind each ear.'

When she was at the end of the lunch line at school, all she had to say was:

'Ladies first, ladies first.'

And she'd get right up to the front of the line. [*Lady smiles victoriously.*]

Well, her life went on like that for quite a while, and she wound up having a pretty good time.

You know, admiring herself in mirrors and always getting to be first in line and stuff like that.

And then one day she went exploring with a whole group of other people through the wilds of the deep and beastly jungle.

As she went along through the tangled trails and the prickly vines, she would say things like: [*indicates each item by pointing*]

'I have *got* to be careful of my lovely dress and my nice white socks and my shiny, shiny shoes and my curly, curly locks, so would somebody *please* clear the way for me?'

And they did.

Or sometimes she'd say:

'What do you mean, there aren't enough mangoes to go around and I'll have to share my mango because I was the last one across that icky river full of crocodiles and snakes? No matter how last I am, it's still "Ladies first, ladies first," so [*harshly*] hand over a whole mango, [*softly, pleasantly*] please.'

And they did.

Well then, guess what happened?

Out of nowhere, the exploring party was seized, grabbed up by a bunch of hungry tigers!

And these tigers tied all the people up and dragged them back to their tiger lair, where they sniffed around, trying to decide what would make the best dinner.

'How about this one?' said the tiger chief.

'Nah, too boney,' said the others.

'Well, what about this one? It's got a lot of meat on it!'

'Uh-uh. Meaty, but muscley.'

'Oh, for heaven's sakes, don't take all night!' said the chief tiger. 'I never saw such a pack of picky eaters. How about this one, then?'

Looks tender … smells nice. In fact I never saw anything quite like it before. I wonder what it is?'

'I am a tender, sweet young thing.'

'Oh, far out,' said the tiger chief.

'I am also a little lady. You should know that by my lovely clothes and my lovely smell.

And if it's all the same to you, Tiger Tweetie, I wish you'd stop licking me.

And untie me this instant! My dress is getting mussed.'

'Yes … uh …' the tiger said. 'Well, as a matter of fact, we were all just … uh … trying to decide who to untie first.'

'Ladies first! Ladies first!' she said. And so she was.

And mighty tasty, too.

From Free To Be … You And Me *by Shel Silverstein*

Writing a script

You can write and perform your own text. Scripts can be developed by:

- brainstorming words or phrases around a topic or theme (a mind map or topic web)
- writing conversations
- using your own short stories or other published stories
- writing your own script.

Theme scripts

  Task 8

In this task you will:

- work in small groups
- create and perform a text using Reader's Theatre.

1 Select a topic or theme, for example, Christmas, a football or rugby match, friendship, a new school, rivers, etc.
2 Work in small groups and brainstorm a list or topic web of everything about the topic or theme.
3 Group or categorise ideas from the web or list.
4 Assign parts for readers.
5 Draft and revise the script.
6 Consider any props or sound effects that will add to the script.
7 Practise and rehearse the final script.
8 Listen to the opinions of others, try to reach agreement and review work at the end.
9 Perform. (Music stands needed for scripts.)

Adapting a story

 Task 9

In this task you will:

- rehearse and present a Reader's Theatre.

1 Select a short story, or an extract from a story.
2 Underline the names of the characters.
3 Add any necessary narrator(s).
4 Draft and revise the script.
5 Highlight each character's and narrator's lines on their copies.
6 Agree on props or sound effects.
7 Rehearse and present the Reader's Theatre.

When writing out your script, do not forget the rules and conventions for the layout and punctuation of a drama text.

Unit review

Here you will:

- review and evaluate what has been understood.

What do you think you have learned in this unit? Discuss the following in pairs (or small groups), or write responses in your Writing Portfolio:

- What skills does a reader need in Reader's Theatre?
- What are your thoughts about the benefits and disadvantages involved in working as a team?
- How is Reader's Theatre different from and similar to formal drama?
- What have you learned about adverbs and adverb phrases?
- What else have you learned?

Unit 6: Using the plot

What we will be doing

In this unit we will:

- read and comment on writers' choice of words, plot, setting and characterisation
- look at the typical features of the genre of detective fiction writing
- develop a questioning approach to texts
- write creatively in the style of detective fiction.

What we will be learning

In this unit we will learn to:

- write, using language for effect
- structure narratives for different purposes
- appreciate aspects of plot development and resolution.

Thinking skills and personal capabilities

In this unit we will:

- read for meaning
- explore explicit and implicit meaning and make inferences and deductions
- develop and justify personal opinions
- organise opinions and ideas clearly
- make connections in your reading and writing
- express opinions and ideas clearly
- develop the ability to ask and answer questions.

Introduction

This unit will show you how to read and write stories focusing on the narrative structure.

Writers have many things to think about as they write their stories. One of the first decisions is working out the **plot** – the sequence of events. At the centre of a good story is a good plot. For readers, it may be good because it is unpredictable, scary, or perhaps romantic. In Unit 2, you looked at different types of reading and fiction. Some of these have typical features that make them recognisable as a particular genre.

> **Glossary**
>
> **Plot** – the plan of a story, its sequence of events

Back to the plot…

What is the plot of the story? What does it mean when we say someone has 'lost the plot'? The plot is the plan, the sequence of events or the structure of the narrative. What happens during the course of a story is the writer's choice. You could think of the writer as the driver of the story car and the reader as the passenger. The writer decides where to go and whether to take the reader on a rocky ride or a smooth one.

Task 1: Plotline of a famous story

In this task you will:

*   think about endings of stories and consider alternatives.

If you look at a familiar story like the children's fable, *Goldilocks and the Three Bears*, you can see what the plot looks like in a sequence of blocks.

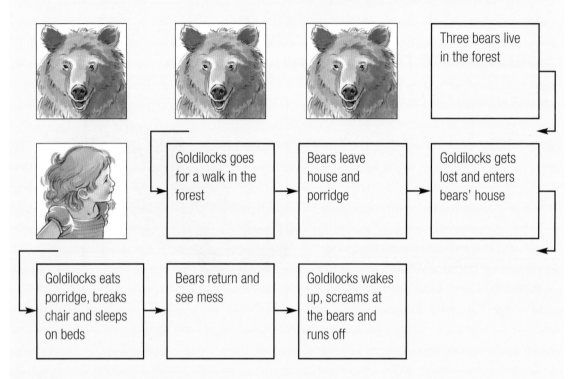

Think about these questions about the plot and the ending:

1   What do you think of the writer's plot?

2   Do you like the ending?

3   What other ending could you choose?

4   Discuss the plot with a partner and act it out for the class, or **freeze frame** the whole story.

Note

A small group freezes in order to represent the action or emotions of a particular situation. Meaning is being made by facial expressions, positions and relationships

Detective or mystery fiction

For the rest of the unit, the learning focus is on the genre of **detective fiction**. This genre has a particular type of plot structure. It is popular for books and for television programmes. You may have seen examples like 'Morse', 'Taggart', 'Dalziel and Pascoe' and 'Buffy the Vampire Slayer' on TV. Why do you think they are so popular?

The key features of detective stories are the twists and turns of the plots with a build-up of tension for the reader. The writer's aim is to keep the reader in suspense about whether the crime will be solved and to find out if the detective is cleverer than the villain. Sometimes clues are left for the reader, who can try to work out the mystery along with the main character.

The shape of the plot

The simplest story starts with everything being all right. Then events happen that build the story. A **complication** produces a problem or **dilemma**. The rest of the story is about solving this, maybe in a series of **resolutions**.

Detective or mystery stories often have exciting **cliff-hangers** – points in the story where the main character or detective is left in deadly danger. The shape of this type of plot is like a series of hills to walk up and down. Or it is like a car journey that takes many sharp turns.

> ### Glossary
> **Cliff-hanger** – a point of build-up in the tension, with no likely solution
> **Complication** – something that causes the main character a problem
> **Dilemma** – the problem to solve
> **Resolution** – the solving of the problem

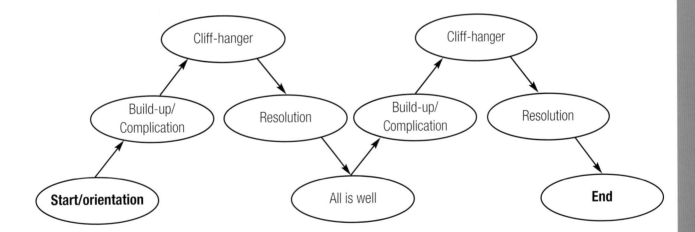

Reading focus

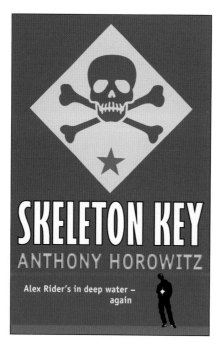

Skeleton Key by Anthony Horowitz

Anthony Horowitz has written a detective/spy novel for young people. The central character, Alex Rider, is a spy, a 12-year-old spy. Alex has a series of adventures that leaves the reader holding his breath.

In Skeleton Key, the third book in the series, the outline of the plot of the first three chapters could be modelled as shown below, by imagining the writer's notes. The features of the plot and characterisation of a **detective** novel have been highlighted.

Chapter One

In the dark 2 meanings

Location: Skeleton Key – remote country, dangerous terrain – typical setting/contrast with 'respectable' Wimbledon later

Description of enemy: Russian often a foreigner, facial features include a scar important to identify him, earlier fights?

Establish crime: illegal handover of uranium for money

Coded warning message: 'I hope you enjoy the flight!'

Build up tension: plane crash – into crocodile water – more than 1 risk

Cliff-hanger statement: 'His target was the entire world.' – to keep reader hooked

---

Chapter Two

Match point climax in match

Introduce hero: Alex Rider

Establish background for new readers: sum up previous missions – to whet the appetite for new readers

Key quote: 'I'm a schoolboy, I'm not a spy!' – some links with the readers

Describe crime: scene – Wimbledon; cover/disguise – ball-boy; strange events – typical of a spy to be in disguise

Add clues for reader: the break-in, good players playing badly

Describe enemy: a strange security guard, behaving suspiciously; description – tattoos, foreign accent – typical

Chapter Three

Blood and strawberries surprising contrast – clues

Add typical spy details: interest in model of mobile/gadgets – think of James Bond and his gadgets

Lure hero into a trap: off the beaten track, alone under the main tennis courts …

Read now what happens next in Chapter Three. As you read, think about how the writer has increased the tension by the way he has written.

Skeleton Key (extract 1)

For the first time since he had left the Complex, Alex played back the telephone conversation in his mind.

I'm going to meet him now. Yes … straight away. He'll give it to me …

It sounded ridiculous, fake, like something out of a bad film. Even as Alex realized this and knew that he had been tricked, he heard the screaming sound, saw the dark shape rushing out of the shadows. He was in the middle of the concrete floor, out in the open. The guard was behind the wheel of a fork-lift truck, the metal prongs jutting out towards him like the horns of an enormous bull. Powered by its forty-eight volt electric engine, the truck was speeding towards him on pneumatic tyres. Alex glanced up and saw the heavy wooden pallets, a dozen of them, balanced high above the cabin. He saw the guard's smile, a gleam of ugly teeth in an uglier face. The truck covered the distance between them with astonishing speed then came to a sudden halt as the guard slammed on the brake. Alex yelled and threw himself to one side. The wooden pallets, carried forward by the truck's momentum, slid off the forks and came clattering down. Alex should have been crushed, would have been, but for the beer barrels. A line of them had taken the weight of the pallets, leaving a tiny triangle of space. Alex heard the wood smashing centimetres above his head. Splinters rained down on his neck and back. Dust and dirt smothered him. But he was still alive. Choking and half blinded, he crawled forward as the fork-lift truck reversed and prepared to come after him again.

How could he have been so stupid? The guard had seen him that first time in the Complex, when he had made his telephone call. Alex had stood there, gaping at the tattoo on the man's arm and had thought that his ballboy uniform would be enough to protect him. And then, in the Millennium Building, Alex had clumsily knocked into him to get his hands on the mobile phone. Of course the guard had known who he was and what he was doing. It didn't matter that he was a teenager. He was dangerous. He had to be taken out.

And so he had laid a trap so obvious that it wouldn't have fooled … well, a schoolboy. Alex might want to think of himself as some sort of superspy who had twice saved the whole world, but that was nonsense. The guard had made a fake phone call and tricked Alex into following him into this desolate area. And now he was going to kill him. It wouldn't matter who he was or how much he had found out once he was dead.

From Skeleton Key *by Anthony Horowitz*

Task 2: Reading detail

In this task you will:

- discuss plot in narrative.

Look at the outline and the extract from *Skeleton Key* opposite.

1   Which two clues had Alex missed? Look closely in paragraph two (the lines in italics).

2   Pick out/underline the description of the enemy. What language features (nouns, verbs, adjectives, etc.) has the writer used to describe the enemy?

Writer's style: aspects of the writing features of detective genre

3   How has the writer, Anthony Horowitz, described the action of the fight to increase the tension? You should look at sentence length and figurative language.

4   Look closely at the language of the last two paragraphs in the extract, the word order and the punctuation. What are the main thoughts of the character?

5   Why do you think that the writer chose to use a long paragraph for the fight and two shorter paragraphs for the character's thoughts?

6   What do you think of the character Alex Rider?

The next extract is from a few pages later in the same book, to show how the writer resolves the crisis and moves the story on from the cliff-hanger.

Skeleton Key (extract 2)

He had only seconds to spare. He knew that the guard would be coming after him and next time he would finish it. He'd had enough. Alex looked left and right. He saw the cylinders of compressed gas and dragged one out of its wire frame. The cylinder seemed to weigh a ton but Alex was desperate. He wrenched the tap on and heard the gas jetting out. Then, holding the cylinder in front of him with both hands, he stepped forward. At that moment, the guard appeared round the side of the fridge. Alex jerked forward, his muscles screaming, shoving the cylinder into the man's face. The gas exploded into the man's eyes, temporarily blinding him. Alex brought the cylinder down, then up again. The metal rim clanged into the guard's head, just above his nose. Alex felt the jolt of solid steel against bone. The guard reeled back. Alex took another step forward. This time he swung the cylinder like a cricket bat, hitting the man with incredible force in the shoulders and neck. The guard never had a chance. He didn't even cry out as he was thrown off his feet and sent hurtling forward into the open fridge.

Alex dropped the cylinder and groaned. It felt as if his arms had been wrenched out of their sockets. His head was still spinning and he wondered if his nose had been broken. He limped forward and looked into the fridge.

There was a curtain of plastic sheets and behind it a mountain of cardboard boxes, each and every one of them filled to the brim with strawberries. Alex couldn't help smiling. Strawberries and cream was one of Wimbledon's greatest traditions, served at crazy prices in the kiosks and restaurants above ground. This was where they were stored. The guard had landed in the middle of the boxes, crushing many of them. He was unconscious, half buried in a blanket of strawberries, his head resting on a bright red pillow of them. Alex stood in the doorway, leaning on the frame for support, allowing the cold air to wash over him. There was a thermostat next to him. Outside the weather was hot. The strawberries had to be kept chilled.

He took one last look at the man who had tried to kill him.

'Out cold,' he said.

Then he reached out and twisted the thermostat control, sending the temperature down below zero.

Out colder.

He closed the fridge door and limped painfully away.

From Skeleton Key *by Anthony Horowitz*

Task 3: Back to the plot

In this task you will:

- make comparisons.

Thinking about the options

1   What do you think of the writer's resolution, compared with your ideas for the plot?

2   Having compared your ideas of the plot development with those of Anthony Horowitz's, now compare the author with another writer of detective fiction, Carolyn Keene.

Reading focus

Nancy Drew mysteries have been published for many years, and are still being written. The author, Carolyn Keene, has created a detective who is also young – Nancy Drew. She is an American teenager who becomes involved in all sorts of difficult situations, which she solves with the help of her two friends, Bess and George.

In the following extract, Nancy is trying to solve the mystery of who has been setting up practical jokes to put off the players in her boyfriend's basketball team. She has broken into the sports complex to check out the locker of the person she suspects.

The Nancy Drew Files: Two Points to Murder

Fortunately, Mike kept an ordinary padlock on his locker. Nancy could crack simple combination locks with no problem, but key types were easier. She drew her lockpick from her pocket and quietly went to work.

She had it open in less than a minute. Mike had the usual assortment of junk in his locker: towels, uniform, sneakers, hand weights, knee brace, ointments, and a sports magazine. He also had an envelope that contained two thousand dollars in twenty-dollar bills, and a list of Emerson's opponents. Beside each one was a negative number: -10, -14, -6, -17 …

What did the numbers mean? Nancy hadn't the slightest idea. She was positive about one thing, though: Mike was up to no good!

Suddenly she froze. Footsteps were coming down the hall!

She had to hide. Glancing around quickly, she noticed several old, unused locker sections against one wall. Should she slip into one of those? No, she decided. It would be a tight squeeze and they might not open from the inside. Where then? The showers?

She spotted a better place – the sauna! Darting across the room, she pulled open its wooden door and zipped inside. Through the narrow window in the door, she saw the lights in the locker room come on.

Nancy shrank back against an interior wall, her heart racing. Too late, she realized that she had forgotten to shut Mike's locker! Oh well. There was nothing she could do about that now. If she was lucky the security guard – or whoever – would think that Mike himself had forgotten to close it. Swallowing hard, she held still and listened.

Outside there was silence. Then some bumping and scraping began. It sounded as if equipment was being moved around, but she couldn't be sure. Who was it? A janitor mopping floors? Nancy remained motionless as several loud clunks sounded right outside the sauna door.

Finally, after what seemed like hours, there was silence again. The window in the sauna's door went dark, indicating that the locker room lights had been turned off.

Relieved, Nancy waited for a minute, and then went to the sauna door to leave. It wouldn't budge. She pushed harder, but still the door wouldn't open. It was blocked from the outside!

Not only that, Nancy realized – the sauna was beginning to get warm! Whoever it was had cranked up the thermostat. She was trapped!

From Two Points to Murder *by Carolyn Keene*

Task 4: Pros, cons and decisions

In this task you will:

- explore further features of detective fiction.

1 Read the text on the opposite page and think about how it compares with the *Skeleton Key* texts. Focus on the features of detective fiction that you have identified.

2 Using a grid like the one below as an outline, compare the features of the texts from the two books, *Skeleton Key* and *Two Points to Murder*.

	Skeleton Key	Two Points to Murder
Main character/ Detective		
Setting		
Plot resolution		
Writer's style		

3 Which text would you like to read more of and why?

Task 5: Questioning

In this task you will:

- think about what you have learned
- do further reading.

If you could ask a writer of detective fiction questions about their novels, what would you ask them? Imagine you could interview Anthony Horowitz about his books. Make up some questions to ask him. Think about what you have learned about how he has crafted his stories and create questions about that, or about his planning, where he gets his plots from, or anything else you think is relevant or interesting.

Further reading

If you are interested in reading more detective fiction, there are many authors to choose from. Check your library for these and others:

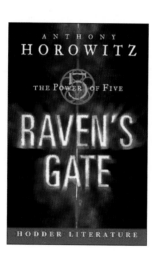

John Buchan, Agatha Christie, Wilkie Collins, Arthur Conan Doyle, Anthony Horowitz, Carolyn Keene, Alexander McCall Smith, Christopher Pike, Edgar Allen Poe, Dorothy L. Sayers, R. L. Stine.

Task 6: ICT – detectives on the web

In this task you will:

- think about the traditional image of a detective.

1 What is the usual image of a detective?

2 If you type the word 'detective' into an internet search engine, you will come up with many images and references to the most famous detective in fiction, Sherlock Holmes, created in the early twentieth century by Arthur Conan Doyle. Investigate this character yourself and see if you can find out these things about him: his usual appearance, clothes, side-kick and key phrases. There are clues in this drawing.

Task 7: Writing

In this task you will:

- write a detective story.

Now it is your turn to write a detective story, or a spy story, or a thriller. Having analysed the writing of other crime writers, you should now be able to:

- create a plot line with twists and turns
- build up tension in your writing
- create a detective with unusual features
- place your character in an appropriate setting.

Step 1: Planning

Decide which direction your plot is going in.

- What is the mystery/crime: any background detail?
- Who saw it?
- Who is going to solve it? How were they brought in?
- What are the clues and how are they revealed?
- What are the main cliff-hangers?
- How are they solved/followed up?
- What happens next?

Some starter ideas for your plot

- Beginning with a court room, someone is accused of a crime.
- Something valuable has been stolen.
- An important public figure has gone missing.
- A family hear an unusual sound that they can't identify.
- Someone takes your photo and when it's developed there is a stranger in the background – who is it?

1   Draw a plotline of what is going to happen using blocks like the outline of the Goldilocks story on page 78 or the illustration on page 79.

2   Draw or write a profile of your detective.

Step 2: Use writing framework
Framework

Paragraph 1 Try to create a sense of mystery
- Where is the action happening? How does your main character feel?
- Decide on the time of day/year/add seasonal hints.
- Why is your character there?
- Create something unusual for the opening (possibly ominous).

Paragraph 2 Build up the tension
- Add a complication to the opening scene, or make everything seem normal, to add to the suspense.
- Introduce another character.
- Add another clue to the mystery (it might be a red herring).

Paragraph 3 Introduce a cliff-hanger

Paragraph 4 Place your detective in a dangerous situation

Paragraph 5 Reveal the solution/resolution

Paragraph 6 Relief/How have the characters reacted?

Step 3: Writing your first draft

Begin with the opening paragraph, which is very important for this kind of story. Check it with your writing partner or your teacher and then continue the story, using the framework, or your own model.

Step 4: Submit your first draft

When you get the first draft back from your writing partner or your teacher, you will be able to see what another reader thinks about how the story is created and developed. They will give you feedback on your setting, characters and plot. Take account of what they have suggested and try out a few alternatives.

Step 5: Redraft and submit again

When you are really happy with the changes you have made, and the technical aspects such as spelling and grammar, submit your best attempt.

Add the finished piece to your Writing Portfolio.

Unit review

Here you will:

- review what you have learned in this unit.

By the end of this unit, you should have learned the following:

- The key features of a detective novel – characterisation, setting, language, plot pattern.
- How to write this genre of text.
- How to draft and redraft to improve writing.
- How to consider different options when writers make choices.
- How to give your opinion on how different writers have developed a plot.

Are you losing or using the plot?

How well have you managed? What do you need to spend more time on?

Unit 7: Toil and trouble

What we will be doing

In this we we will:

- read extracts from the play Macbeth which was written by Shakespeare
- talk and listen to others talk about the play
- dramatise parts of the play
- write in response to the play.

What we will be learning

In this unit we will learn to:

- work independently, managing your own time
- set and work towards personal targets
- evaluate your work and your learning.

Thinking skills and personal capabilities

In this unit we will:

- ask deeper and wider questions to clarify the task, to plan and to set goals
- explain and justify methods, opinions and conclusions
- learn from and build on own and others' ideas and experiences.

Macbeth

  Task 1

In this task you will:

- consider a range of objects linked to the play
- discuss ideas about what these objects tell us about the story.

1   What do the objects in the illustration above suggest might happen in the play of 'Macbeth'?

2   How do you think the objects are linked?

Three Witches

The play begins on a remote heath where three witches are huddled together:

[Thunder and lightning. Enter three witches]

First witch:	When shall we three meet again
	In thunder, lightning, or in rain?
Second witch:	When the hurlyburly's done,
	When the battle's lost and won.
Third witch:	That will be ere the set of sun.
First witch:	Where the place?
Second witch:	Upon the heath.
Third witch:	There to meet with Macbeth.
ALL:	Fair is foul, and foul is fair:
	Hover through the fog and filthy air.

Glossary

Ere – before
Hurlyburly – loud noise or confusion

Did you know?

When Shakespeare wrote his plays people believed in witches and their magical powers. Every year many innocent women lost their lives as they were suspected of being witches.

Task 2

In this task you will:

- answer questions based on your reading
- share your ideas on staging this scene.

1   Shakespeare introduces the witches in the very first scene of 'Macbeth'. What effect might this have upon the audience?

2   What do the witches mean when they say, 'Fair is foul, and foul is fair'?

3   Why do you think the witches want to meet with Macbeth?

4   In small groups, work on presenting this scene. Consider:
- how the witches will enter
- how the witches speak
- how the witches look
- how the witches react to each other.

Brave Macbeth

In the next scene, the action moves to an army camp. We find out that Scotland is at war with Norway. A wounded sergeant approaches from the battlefield to tell Duncan, the King of Scotland, about a very brave soldier called Macbeth.

For brave Macbeth (well he deserves that name),
… with his brandished steel,
Which smoked with bloody execution
… carved out his passage
Till he faced the slave;
Which ne'er shook hands, nor bade farewell to him,
Till he unseam'd him from the nave to the chaps,
And fixed his head upon our battlements.

Glossary

Brandished – to wave about
Chaps – the jaws
Nave – the navel
Unseamed – to tear apart

 Task 3

In this task you will:

- discuss your first impressions of Macbeth.

1   What does Macbeth do when he meets his enemy?
2   What is your impression of Macbeth after learning about his behaviour during battle?

The witches meet Macbeth

In the next scene, we finally meet 'brave Macbeth'. The war is over and Scotland is victorious. King Duncan decides to reward Macbeth for his bravery by giving him a new title, 'The Thane of Cawdor'. Macbeth is already known by the title 'Thane of Glamis'.

Macbeth is riding home from battle with his friend Banquo when they see the witches on the heath.

Glossary

Thane – a title given to a Scottish aristocrat
Get – to be the father of

First witch:	All hail, Macbeth! Hail, to thee, Thane of Glamis!
Second witch:	All hail, Macbeth! Hail to thee, Thane of Cawdor!
Third witch:	All hail, Macbeth! That shalt be king hereafter!
Witches (*to Banquo*):	Lesser than Macbeth, and greater
	Thou shalt get kings, though thou be none.

 Task 4

In this task you will:

* answer questions based on your reading of the text.

1   What three titles do the witches greet Macbeth with?
2   Which title do you and the audience already know he is about to be given? Which title might surprise them?
3   In your own words, explain the witches' predictions for Banquo.

Macbeth and his friend Banquo are confused and shocked at meeting these three strange women. Then, just at the moment the witches vanish, the King's men arrive to tell Macbeth he has been awarded a new title, Thane of Cawdor.

Task 5

In this task you will:

- work in pairs to write questions you would like to ask the characters in the play.

In pairs, think about what questions you would like to ask Macbeth and Banquo after their experience with the witches.

Macbeth writes home

  Task 6

In this task you will:

- plan, write and review your writing.

Macbeth decides to write a letter to his wife to tell her he is on his way home from war and to inform her that a guest, King Duncan, is coming to stay with them. Write Macbeth's letter.

Plan your work

Think about what Macbeth might want to include in this letter. Here are some suggestions:

- His experiences in the bloody war against Norway.
- The three witches on the heath and their prophecies.
- Macbeth's new title, The Thane of Cawdor.
- News that King Duncan is coming to stay at Macbeth's castle.

Review your work

- How did you plan your writing?
- Did you revise or redraft your work?
- Did you achieve what you set out to do?
- What could be improved?

Shakespeare's language

One of the things you may have noticed about the play is that the language used is different from the language you use.

- What are the main differences?
- Can you think of reasons for these differences?

Shakespeare and the Elizabethans loved language. The average Elizabethan would have had about 20,000 words in his or her vocabulary; the average person today has around 4000. Shakespeare himself introduced many new words and phrases into the language. Perhaps you have heard some of them before; *barefaced*, *obscene*, *vanish into thin air*, *being cruel to be kind* and *slept not one wink* are just a few.

Many of the words used by Elizabethans are no longer used today. Think yourself lucky that some of them have disappeared, such as 'honorificabilitudinatibus'. Can you guess what this word means?

  Task 7

In this task you will:

- consider with a partner the language you use every day and how it changes over time.

In pairs, discuss the following points.

- Why do we stop using some words?
- Which words do you think will no longer be used in 100 years' time (for example, *video*, *petrol*, *texting*)?

Lady Macbeth

When Lady Macbeth receives Macbeth's letter, she speaks aloud to herself; this is called a **soliloquy.** Why do you think characters on stage do this?

> **Glossary**
>
> **Soliloquy** – type of speech spoken by one character when alone on stage. It is used to communicate the character's thoughts and feelings to the audience

Lady Macbeth:	Glamis thou art, and Cawdor; and shalt be
	What thou art promis'd. Yet I do fear thy nature;
	It is too full o' the milk of human kindness
	Art not without ambition, but without
	The illness that should attend it …
	Hie thee hither,
	That I may pour my spirits in thine ear.

Task 8

In this task you will:

- respond to the text
- discuss your impressions of Lady Macbeth.

1. Below is a jumbled up, modern-day version of the lines Lady Macbeth speaks. Working in pairs, arrange them in the correct order.
   - I want to tell you of my evil plans.
   - Come here soon.
   - You have the ambition to be King but you are not evil enough to do anything about it.
   - I am afraid that you are far too nice.
   - You are Thane of Glamis, and now Cawdor, and you will also be king as predicted.

2. Does Lady Macbeth's view of her husband match the view that the King and other members of the army have of him?

3. What are your first impressions of Lady Macbeth? Which of the following images do you think is most suitable?

4. Draw your own picture of how you think Lady Macbeth might look.

The plan to kill the King

When Macbeth arrives home, he tells his wife that they are going to have a visitor stay with them that evening, the King. Lady Macbeth immediately sees this as an opportunity for Macbeth to fulfil his destiny and become King. In order to do this, she believes he will have to murder the King. She advises him to, 'Look like the innocent flower but be the serpent under it'.

Did you know?

In Shakespeare's times people believed in the 'Divine Right of Kings'. This meant they believed the King was chosen directly by God to rule over their country. Therefore, to kill a king was not only a crime but also a very serious sin against God.

 # Task 9

In this task you will:

- consider two different approaches to a problem.

1   Put yourself in Macbeth's position: should you kill the King? To help you decide, draw up a list of reasons for and against murdering King Duncan. One has been completed for you.

For	Against
I could become King	He is my friend

2   Which do you think has the stronger arguments – for or against?

After some consideration, Macbeth decides he should not kill the King.

His wife is not very happy when she hears this.

  # Task 10

In this task you will:

- write a script.

In pairs, write a script for the conversation Macbeth and Lady Macbeth have about whether or not he should kill the King. Remember, Lady Macbeth wants her husband to kill the King, so what will she say to try to persuade him?

Reporter's notebook

- *King Duncan brutally **murdered** as he slept*
- *He was spending the night at Inverness – Macbeth's castle*
- *Cause of death – **multiple stab wounds to the chest**.*

*Main suspects are the King's guards (find out their names); they were found asleep outside the bedroom, their knives smeared with the King's blood. **What was their motivation?** Could have been drunk. A servant said, 'They were drinking all evening'. Another possibility – working for the King of Norway?*

***Macduff,** Thane of Fife, discovered the body (interview him). Why was he there? What did he discover in the King's bedroom? What did he do?*

*A servant said '**Lady Macbeth fainted** when she heard the news'.*

Macbeth killed the guards in a fit of rage. Then he said, 'Who can be wise, amazed, temperate and furious, loyal and neutral, in a moment?'

The guards are dead, will we now ever find out the truth?

*The King's sons, **Malcolm** and **Donalbain**, left Inverness quickly after they heard the news. A servant is reported to have heard Malcolm say 'Where we are there's daggers in men's smiles'. Was it safer for them to leave than stay?*

*With Malcolm and Donalbain gone – **who shall be King**?*

Our recent war means a strong King is needed. Who can do this job?

*The Thanes are to **meet this evening** to elect a new King.*

Task 11

In this task you will:

* plan, write and review your writing.

Use the notes from the reporter's notebook opposite to piece together what has happened. Then write the newspaper story for *The Scottish Times*.

Planning

* What is the purpose of a newspaper report?
* Who is the audience?
* How will you structure your report?

The King is dead. Long live the King!

With Malcolm and Donalbain gone, Macbeth is elected Scotland's new King. However, Macbeth and Lady Macbeth do not live happily ever after; one person has his doubts …

> **Banquo:** Thou hast it now: King, Cawdor, Glamis, all,
> As the weird women promised. And I fear
> Thou played most foully for it.

Macbeth knows Banquo's suspicions could be dangerous for him. To make sure Banquo does not cause him any problems, Macbeth hires two murderers to kill his friend and Banquo's son, Fleance.

  Task 12

In this task you will:

* discuss your thoughts on the characters in the play.

1   Which act is worse: killing the King or killing your best friend?
2   What are your opinions of Macbeth at this stage of the play?
3   Has Macbeth's character changed in any way?
4   Choose three adjectives you would use to describe Macbeth.

The banquet

On the evening Banquo is murdered, Macbeth holds a feast to celebrate his coronation. However, all does not go as planned. In the middle of the banquet, Macbeth looks around to see the ghost of his murdered friend, Banquo, sitting on one of the stools.

Glossary

Avaunt – go away

Coronation – the ceremony of crowning a new king

Foully – unfairly

Gory locks – bloody hair

The order of your going – the idea that the most important people should be allowed to leave first

Macbeth:	Which of you have done this?
Lords:	What, my good lord?
Macbeth (*to the ghost*):	Never shake thy gory locks at me.
	Avaunt and quit my sight!
	Let the earth hide thee!
	Hence, horrible shadow!
Lady Macbeth (*to the lords*):	I pray you, speak not; he grows worse and worse.
	At once, good-night.
	Standnot upon the order of your going,
	But go at once.

  Task 13

In this task you will:

* work in groups to present a role play.

In groups, adopt the roles of one of the lords. You gather together after the banquet to discuss the actions of your new King that evening.

1 What are your thoughts on what you saw?

2 Consider how Macbeth and his wife acted. How do you feel about this?

3 Was anyone missing from the gathering of lords?

Macbeth visits the witches

After the experience at the banquet, Macbeth is feeling very uncertain about his position as King. He decides to visit the witches. When Macbeth asks them to predict his future, this is what the witches say:

Witches:　　Round about the cauldron go,
　　　　　　　In the poisoned entrails throw.
　　　　　　　Speak. Demand. We'll answer.

[First apparition of a head wearing a helmet]
　　　　　　　Macbeth! Macbeth! Beware Macduff!

[Second apparition of a blood-smeared child]
　　　　　　　Be bloody, bold and resolute, for none of woman born
　　　　　　　Shall harm Macbeth.

[Third apparition of a child wearing a crown, with a tree in his hand]
　　　　　　　Be lion-mettled, proud and take no care;
　　　　　　　Macbeth shall never vanquished be until
　　　　　　　Great Birnam wood to high Dunsinane hill
　　　　　　　Shall come against him.

Glossary

Apparition – a ghostly figure
Entrails – the internal organs, usually of an animal
Resolute – to stand strong against your enemy
Vanquished – defeated or conquered

Task 14

In this task you will:

- draw and answer questions based on your reading.

1   Draw the three apparitions described in the previous extract.
2   Beside each drawing write the advice the witches give to accompany the apparitions.
3   What might Macbeth think these apparitions mean for his future?
4   What do you think Macbeth will do next?

Macbeth is wrong to feel confident about his position as King. He is unpopular among his subjects and Malcolm, the old King's son, has been working with an English Lord to organise an army to march on Scotland.

News that Malcolm and the English army are marching to Scotland to try and overthrow Macbeth reaches Dunsinane castle, where Macbeth now lives. When a messenger tells him that the troops are fast approaching, he says:

Macbeth:	Bring me no more reports: let them fly all:
	Till Birnam wood remove to Dunsinane
	I cannot taint with fear.
	I'll fight till from my bones my flesh be hacked.

Task 15

In this task you will:

- work in pairs to present a speech from the play.

1   In what way would Macbeth say the speech on the previous page?
    What emotions would be evident?

2   In pairs, practise different ways of performing Macbeth's speech. Is he
    angry, confident, arrogant, nervous, exhausted or depressed?

Glossary

Camouflage – to conceal or hide yourself from view

Meanwhile, in a field not too far away from Dunsinane, Malcolm tells his soldiers to camouflage themselves with branches from Birnam Wood. This makes it look as though Birnam Wood is on the move.

  Task 16

In this task you will:

- think about what you have read so far
- predict what might happen next.

1 Think back to the witches' third apparition. How did Macbeth interpret it?

2 What has actually happened?

3 What do you think might happen next?

The end for Lady Macbeth

Lady Macbeth is now full of remorse for her part in killing King Duncan. She starts to sleepwalk and she constantly scrubs her hands trying to get rid of an imaginary stain. She is heard to say 'Out damned spot, out.' Unable to go on any longer, she takes her own life.

  Task 17

In this task you will:

- write imaginatively, setting yourself a personal target to improve upon.

Write the last entry in Lady Macbeth's diary.

Plan your work

- Consider what the purpose of a diary entry is.
- Remember you have to write in character.
- Were Lady Macbeth's thoughts collected or confused?

Personal target

Before beginning this task, make a note of a personal target you would like to achieve. For example, checking your work for spelling and punctuation mistakes, adding more detail to your writing, or anything else you would like to improve. After you have finished, review your work.

The battle

Meanwhile, Macbeth prepares to meet Malcolm's army. Even though his men are deserting him, Macbeth decides to stay and fight. He appears quite unmoved when he hears the news of his wife's death. Why do you think this might be?

Macbeth fights bravely, believing that he cannot be defeated. He remembers the witches' words: 'No man of woman born shall harm Macbeth'. This gives him confidence.

 Task 18

In this task you will:

- offer solutions to Macbeth's problems.

You are Macbeth's chief adviser. Use this table to come up with a plan to help him out of the situation in which he finds himself. Copy and complete the grid below and use it to find solutions for Macbeth.

Cause	Problem	Solution
	• The Thanes are fleeing. • The English army is approaching Dunsinane. • The forest appears to be 'moving'.	

Hail, King of Scotland

The British troops led by Malcolm are advancing towards Dunsinane where Macbeth remains. Cleverly disguised as Birnam Wood, they finally manage to storm Macbeth's castle.

Inside, Macbeth, dressed in his full armour, awaits them. Most of his thanes have deserted him. He fights some of the advancing troops until he is confronted by a former friend, the thane of Fife, Macduff. Macduff has good reason to hate Macbeth as Macbeth recently ordered the murder of Macduff's wife and children.

Macbeth:	They have tied me to a stake; I cannot fly,
	But bear-like I must fight the course. What's he
	That was not born of woman?
Macduff:	Tyrant show thy face.
	If thou be slain and with no stroke of mine,
	My wife and children's ghosts will haunt me still.
	Turn, hell hound, turn!
Macbeth:	I bear a charmed life, which must not yield
	To one of woman born.
Macduff:	Macduff was from his mother's womb untimely ripped.

[The two men fight and then Macduff kills Macbeth]

Macduff (*to Malcolm*):   Hail, king of Scotland!

Glossary

From his mother's womb untimely ripped – he was born by caesarean section
Slain – violently murdered
Tyrant – a powerful but cruel leader

 Task 19

In this task you will:

- answer questions based on your reading.

1 Why might Macduff in particular be keen to seek Macbeth's death?

2 What surprising fact does Macduff tell Macbeth right before he murders him?

3 How do Macduff's comments help to explain the witches' prophecies?

4 How does the audience feel at the end of the play?

5 What points do you think Shakespeare might have been making in this play about:

- good and evil
- loyalty to your King
- the supernatural?

Task 20

In this task you will:

- work in groups to produce a script
- perform and record a radio news bulletin.

1 In groups, plan and then script a radio news report for the evening of Macbeth's death. You have two minutes to fill on air and you must include an interview with those present at the scene of Macbeth's death.

2 Once you have written the script, record your report.

Unit review

Here you will:

- consider what you have learned
- consider what you have done in this unit.

Ask yourself these questions:

- What do you know about Shakespeare and the times he lived in?
- Can you summarise the plot of 'Macbeth'?
- What do you know about the language Shakespeare used?
- What type of writing did you enjoy most in this unit?
- What did you learn about performing scenes from a play?
- When did you work independently?
- What personal targets did you set for yourself?
- What else have you learned about how you manage yourself and your learning?

Unit 8: Reading images

What we will be doing

In this unit we will:

- examine pictures
- work individually, in pairs and in groups
- discuss and share ideas
- create an advertisement
- keep a log
- talk and write about 'thinking'.

What we will be learning

In this unit we will learn:

- that pictures are constructs
- that pictures are texts
- to read picture texts
- that sometimes we must go beyond the literal to secure meaning.

Thinking skills and personal capabilities

In this unit we will:

- work towards personal goals and success criteria identified by yourself and the teacher
- make links between your learning in different contexts
- work with others
- pose questions that do not have straightforward answers
- become more confident in your knowledge of personal strengths and weaknesses.

Reading images

Before you begin this unit, your teacher will encourage you to set personal goals for your learning and to formulate success criteria. When the unit is completed, you will be asked to evaluate what you have done and learned, and to record your strengths and the areas that need improvement.

If you were asked how people communicate with one another, you would probably say through talking, listening, writing and reading, and you would be right!

However, sometimes we communicate without words. Think of a time when a friend raised an eyebrow to you when the teacher's back was turned or the way an Olympic winner raises their joined hands in the air, or the way someone cuddles a baby when it is crying.

  Task 1

In this task you will:

- work with others
- compare and classify.

Glossary

Non-verbal – using no words, either spoken or written

1   In pairs, list and discuss non-verbal ways of communicating. For example, you might consider how pets make their wants known or how you can tell what mood your teacher is in before he or she speaks.

2   Look at the pictures on the following page and decide what mood each person is expressing. Is this difficult to do when the image is static? What clues has the artist given you?

3   The pictures below are all of bears. How do you think the bears are feeling? How do you know? Discuss this in pairs, then join with another pair to compare your ideas.

Did you think of the following things?

- colour
- size
- position
- expression.

Now you have begun to think of the methods an artist might use when constructing an image.

Task 2

In this task you will:

- make connections.

Examine the picture below and answer the questions the teacher will give you.

You now know that people do not always need words to communicate; you know that it is possible to read a picture. So, not all texts have words.

To get the most meaning from a picture, it is good to remind yourself that, like any other text, it has a creator, an audience in mind, and that it was constructed for a purpose.

> **Note**
> A **picture** can be a **text**

Task 3

In this task you will:

- examine a text
- pose questions about the text's construction
- explain and justify your conclusions.

1   Look at the picture your teacher gives you, and then ask yourself these questions:

- What is this text about?
- What type of audience was it made for?
- Who made the text?
- Why?
- How was the text made?
- How do I feel about it?

2   Make notes and then write about your picture.

Task 4

In this task you will:

- work with others
- generate interpretations.

You know that pictures can be used for a variety of purposes. The picture below could have been used in an advertisement for butter. In pairs, answer the following questions in note form.

1   What can be seen in the picture?
2   Why were these things chosen?
3   What are the main colours?
4   What effect do the colours have?
5   What connection does the picture have with butter?
6   Who is the advertisement aimed at?
7   Do you think the advertisement will succeed?

> **Note**
>
> The aim of the advertiser is to make you **feel** a certain way when you look at the images in the advertisement and then **transfer** that feeling to the product

Task 5

In this task you will:

- make ideas real by experimenting with different designs.

1   Create a picture that you could use in an advertisement for a product that would interest teenagers. Make the images you choose add to the effect you want to create.

Remember:

- your picture does not have to relate directly to the product
- the picture should make the viewer think or feel in a particular way
- to think of the lines and spaces in your picture
- to think of the colours and their effect
- to think of the size and position of people and objects in your picture.

2   Use ICT to enhance and produce your picture.

You will be asked to keep a log in which to record your ideas, amendments, progress, thoughts, thinking processes, evaluation of the process and the product. This may be displayed with your advertisement, and then stored in your Writing Portfolio.

  Task 6

In this task you will:

- work in a group
- be willing to critically evaluate ideas and to reassess opinions.

1   Your teacher will give you a painting by a famous artist.
2   'Read' the painting and then report to your group the meanings you took from it.

Task 7

In this task you will:

- use all of your senses to contribute to ideas
- work with others.

1. You will have an opportunity to see some moving images. For these, you can ask the same questions you asked in previous tasks for the still picture texts you have seen. In addition, you might want to examine the effect of:

   - costume
   - music
   - positioning
   - movement
   - camera angle
   - shots
   - sound effects.

2. What thinking skills did you employ?

When we 'read' pictures it is like reading words. We read what we can see in front of us, but we make inferences and connections and can think beyond what is actually in front of us. This is what the artist wants us to do.

By reading and questioning what we see, we develop our own thinking and we may get to the central message of the text.

Task 8

In this task you will:

- pose questions that do not have straightforward answers
- make new connections between ideas and information.

1 As a class, select a picture. Individually, study it and complete the following grid.

I see	I think	I wonder

2 Now choose the most interesting statement from the 'I wonder' column. Turn this into a question and write the question on a card where everyone can see it.

3 In pairs, take time to discuss everyone's question.

4 Decide on a question you would all like to know more about. Spend some time talking it over and noting your responses.

5 Look at the picture again. Have your ideas been strengthened? Have they changed? Did you think of and talk about things not directly connected to the picture?

Each of you will now have an opportunity to speak briefly about what you learned in this activity, and what thinking skills were involved.

Unit review

Here you will:

- review your own work
- recognise your personal strengths and weaknesses.

In this unit how well did you:

- identify what you needed to know?
- set personal goals?
- prioritise?
- persevere?
- use success criteria?
- learn the skills necessary to read pictures?
- recognise other areas where these skills could be used?